STARTINGUP NOW

- - - - - - - - - - - - → 24 Steps To Launch
Your Own Business

↓

FACILITATORGUIDE

L. Brian Jenkins, M.A.
Foreword by Don G. Soderquist
Vice Chairman & COO, Walmart Stores, Inc.

STARTINGUP NOW

"StartingUp is a complete guide for novice and experienced entrepreneurs who know that today they cannot afford to make time-consuming and expensive mistakes, and who are committed to maximizing their chances for success. The guide provides a holistic system of dealing with personal growth issues that are so important for business leaders to deal with, as well as developing key business concepts, and wrapping it around technology that progressive entrepreneurs must be able to navigate."

—Dr. Zira J. Smith, Entrepreneurship & Small Business Educator
University of Illinois-Cook County

"I think you have indeed put together the fundamental steps that a person needs to take in developing a successful business—based on my own experience."

—Dr. Melvin Banks Sr., Founder, Urban Ministries, Inc.

"StartingUp is a new and exciting tool for entrepreneurs of all ages. If you are just starting your business or are a seasoned business owner needing quick answers and easy access, StartingUp is for you. I highly recommend this revolutionary tool."

—Andre Thornton, President & CEO, ASW Global, LLC

"No more excuses! StartingUp Now is your blue print for business creation that will become a lasting resource to turn your idea into your future."

—Jeffrey Weber, Entrepreneur & Author of IDEA to Exit

...continued

iii

STARTINGUP NOW

"The StartingUp Skill Center lets me interact with other students who own their businesses. We share ideas, links, and tips online. I've met people, other kids actually, interested in owning their own business from around the world."
—William, High School Student Business Owner

"StartingUp Now has several useful and beneficial applications. As a business owner for many years and an entrepreneurship education proponent, I highly recommend StartingUp Now as an excellent resource for both those new to business and those who instruct individuals in principles of entrepreneurship. The website is easy to navigate and provides excellent answers to many frequently asked questions relative to business structure. I've read many books on business development and this resource is one of the best new books on the market. As a pastor, I feel this tool will be useful as our board of leaders embark on strategic planning for the ministry."
**—Dr. Hazel A. King, President, H.A. King & Associates, Inc.
Pastor, Greater Faith Ministries International**

"StartingUp Now takes a fresh and modern approach to planning the launch of a business. The bite-size chunks of information, flexible format, and mobile access make this guide more relevant and useful for today's entrepreneurs."
**—Raman Chadha, Executive Director & Clinical Professor
DePaul University, Coleman Entrepreneurship Center**

►ACCLAIM FOR STARTINGUP NOW

"StartingUp Now has helped me tremendously not just as an entrepreneur, but as an individual that believes in destiny and manifestation of ideas through one's individual talents and beliefs. The great thing about entrepreneurship is the idea of creating nothing from something. Entrepreneurship leaves me with no excuses—just limitless opportunities. And StartingUp Now helps all believers in greatness make their dreams a reality."

—Stephan Hall, Entrenuity Alum, Partner
Trash Geeks, Inc.

"Brian has been on the front lines of innovative youth work for almost two decades. StartingUp Now is his life's passion to provide practical, real, transferable principles and skills to train youth and adults to OWN their businesses."

—Phil Jackson, Pastor & Founder of The House Covenant Church
Author: The Hip Hop Church

"Entrepreneurship is a language that needs to be spoken by people everywhere. The StartingUp Now toolkit is an accessible and much-needed on ramp to the world of value creation and self-sustainability."

—Rodolpho Carrasco, U.S. Regional Facilitator,
Partners Worldwide and
Director, Two Forty Group

ISBN-13: 978-0615540962
ISBN-10: 0615540961

The National Content Standards for Entrepreneurship Education and related Toolkit
are the property of the Consortium for Entrepreneurship Education. The Consortium
for Entrepreneurship Education, Columbus, Ohio www.entre-ed.org
Copyright © 2004 by the Consortium for Entrepreneurship Education

Printed in the United States of America

Design by: Kathyjo Varco, Big Sound Music, Inc.
Edited by: Vicki D. Frye, Fryeday Everyday

10 9 8 7 6 5 4 3 2 1

First Edition

DEDICATION

Thank you, Jenai Jenkins—my wife, life-partner, a model mother to my children, and friend. Without your unequivocal support, the experiences learned and shared in this book would not be possible. You are the woman so eloquently defined by Solomon in Proverbs 31:10–31. I also dedicate this book to our children—Bria Nichelle, Lawrence Braxton, and Brooke Elise—who inspire me daily to strive to be the best father I know how to be. I'm still working on it…

To my parents, Larry and Madelyn Jenkins—you define what it means to support and guide your children. Thank you for always being there.

TABLE OF CONTENTS

STARTINGUP NOW

TABLE OF CONTENTS

STARTINGUP NOW

THE NATIONAL CONTENT STANDARDS FOR ENTREPRENEURSHIP EDUCATION

The following section reflects guidelines developed by The Consortium for Entrepreneurship Education. Each StartingUp Now Lesson Plan utilizes these standards as a way to define the processes, traits, and behaviors associated with entrepreneurial success. Use this detailed reference listing as a tool for monitoring your students' progress.

[A] ENTREPRENEURIAL PROCESSES: Understands concepts and processes associated with successful entrepreneurial performance

Discovery
A.01 Explain the need for entrepreneurial discovery
A.02 Discuss entrepreneurial discovery processes
A.03 Assess global trends and opportunities
A.04 Determine opportunities for venture creation
A.05 Assess opportunities for venture creation
A.06 Describe idea-generation methods
A.07 Generate venture ideas
A.08 Determine feasibility of ideas

Concept Development
A.09 Describe entrepreneurial planning considerations
A.10 Explain tools used by entrepreneurs for venture planning
A.11 Assess start-up requirements
A.12 Assess risks associated with venture
A.13 Describe external resources useful to entrepreneurs during concept development
A.14 Assess the need to use external resources for concept development
A.15 Describe strategies to protect intellectual property
A.16 Use components of a business plan to define venture idea

Resourcing
A.17 Distinguish between debt and equity financing for venture creation
A.18 Describe processes used to acquire adequate financial resources for venture creation/start-up
A.19 Select sources to finance venture creation/start-up
A.20 Explain factors to consider in determining a venture's human-resource needs
A.21 Describe considerations in selecting capital resources
A.22 Acquire capital resources needed for the venture
A.23 Assess the costs/benefits associated with resources

Actualization
A.24 Use external resources to supplement entrepreneur's expertise
A.25 Explain the complexity of business operations
A.26 Evaluate risk-taking opportunities
A.27 Explain the need for business systems and procedures
A.28 Describe the use of operating procedures

Actualization (continued)

A.29 Explain methods/processes for organizing work flow

A.30 Develop and/or provide product/service

A.31 Use creativity in business activities/decisions

A.32 Explain the impact of resource productivity on venture success

A.33 Create processes for ongoing opportunity recognition

A.34 Adapt to changes in business environment

Harvesting

A.35 Explain the need for continuation planning

A.36 Describe methods of venture harvesting

A.37 Evaluate options for continued venture involvement

A.38 Develop exit strategies

[B] ENTREPRENEURIAL TRAITS/BEHAVIORS: Understands the personal traits/behaviors associated with successful entrepreneurial performance

Leadership

B.01 Demonstrate honesty and integrity

B.02 Demonstrate responsible behavior

B.03 Demonstrate initiative

B.04 Demonstrate ethical work habits

B.05 Exhibit passion for goal attainment

B.06 Recognize others' efforts

B.07 Lead others using positive statements

B.08 Develop team spirit

B.09 Enlist others in working toward a shared vision

B.10 Share authority, when appropriate

B.11 Value diversity

Personal Assessment

B.12 Describe desirable entrepreneurial personality traits

B.13 Determine personal biases and stereotypes

B.14 Determine interests

B.15 Evaluate personal capabilities

B.16 Conduct self-assessment to determine entrepreneurial potential

Personal Management

B.17 Maintain positive attitude

B.18 Demonstrate interest and enthusiasm

B.19 Make decisions

B.20 Develop an orientation to change

B.21 Demonstrate problem-solving skills

B.22 Assess risks

B.23 Assume personal responsibility for decisions

B.24 Use time-management principles

B.25 Develop tolerance for ambiguity

B.26 Use feedback for personal growth

B.27 Demonstrate creativity

B.28 Set personal goals

Ready Skills

The basic business knowledge and skills that are prerequisites
or co-requisites for becoming a successful entrepreneur.

[C] **BUSINESS FOUNDATIONS:** Understands fundamental business concepts
that affect business decision-making

Business Concepts

C.01 Explain the role of business in society

C.02 Describe types of business activities

C.03 Explain types of businesses

C.04 Explain opportunities for creating added value

C.05 Determine issues and trends in business

C.06 Describe crucial elements of a quality culture/continuous quality improvement

C.07 Describe the role of management in the achievement of quality

C.08 Explain the nature of managerial ethics

C.09 Describe the need for and impact of ethical business practices

Business Activities

C.10 Explain marketing management and its importance in a global economy

C.11 Describe marketing functions and related activities

C.12 Explain the nature and scope of operations management

C.13 Explain the concept of management

C.14 Explain the concept of financial management

Business Activities (continued)

C.15 Explain the concept of human resource management

C.16 Explain the concept of risk management

C.17 Explain the concept of strategic management

[D] COMMUNICATIONS AND INTERPERSONAL SKILLS: Understands concepts, strategies, and systems needed to interact effectively with others

Fundamentals of Communication

D.01 Explain the nature of effective communications

D.02 Apply effective listening skills

D.03 Use proper grammar and vocabulary

D.04 Reinforce service orientation through communication

D.05 Explain the nature of effective verbal communications

D.06 Address people properly

D.07 Handle telephone calls in a businesslike manner

D.08 Make oral presentations

D.09 Explain the nature of written communications

D.10 Write business letters

D.11 Write informational messages

D.12 Write inquiries

D.13 Write persuasive messages

D.14 Prepare simple written reports

D.15 Prepare complex written reports

D.16 Use communications technologies/systems (e.g., e-mail, faxes, voice mail, cell phones, etc.)

Staff Communications

D.17 Follow directions

D.18 Explain the nature of staff communication

D.19 Give directions for completing job tasks

D.20 Conduct staff meetings

Ethics in Communication

D.21 Respect the privacy of others

D.22 Explain ethical considerations in providing information

Group Working Relationships

D.23 Treat others fairly at work

D.24 Develop cultural sensitivity

D.25 Foster positive working relationships

D.26 Participate as a team member

Dealing with Conflict

D.27 Demonstrate self-control

D.28 Show empathy for others

D.29 Use appropriate assertiveness

D.30 Demonstrate negotiation skills

D.31 Handle difficult customers/clients

D.32 Interpret business policies to customers/clients

D.33 Handle customer/client complaints

D.34 Explain the nature of organizational change

D.35 Describe the nature of organizational conflict

D.36 Explain the nature of stress management

[E] DIGITAL SKILLS: Understands concepts and procedures needed for basic computer operations

Computer Basics

E.01 Use basic computer terminology

E.02 Apply basic commands of operating system software

E.03 Employ desktop operating skills

E.04 Determine file organization

E.05 Demonstrate system utilities for file management

E.06 Compress or alter files

E.07 Use reference materials to access information

E.08 Use menu systems

E.09 Use control panel components

E.10 Access data through various computer drives

Computer Applications

E.11 Demonstrate basic search skills on the Web

E.12 Evaluate credibility of Internet resources

E.13 Demonstrate file management skills

E.14 Communicate by computer

E.15 Solve routine hardware and software problems

E.16 Operate computer-related hardware peripherals

E.17 Explain the nature of e-commerce

E.18 Describe the impact of the Internet on business

E.19 Develop basic website

[F] ECONOMICS: Understands the economic principles and concepts fundamental to entrepreneurship/small-business ownership

Basic Concepts

F.01 Distinguish between economic goods and services

F.02 Explain the factors of production

F.03 Explain the concept of scarcity

F.04 Explain the concept of opportunity costs

F.05 Describe the nature of economics and economic activities

F.06 Determine forms of economic utility created by business activities

F.07 Explain the principles of supply and demand

F.08 Describe the concept of price

Cost-Profit Relationships

F.09 Explain the concept of productivity

F.10 Describe cost/benefit analysis

F.11 Analyze the impact of specialization/division of labor on productivity

F.12 Explain the concept of organized labor and business

F.13 Explain the law of diminishing returns

F.14 Describe the concept of economies of scale

Economic Indicators/Trends

F.15 Explain measures used to analyze economic conditions

F.16 Explain the nature of the Consumer Price Index

F.17 Explain the concept of Gross Domestic Product

F.18 Determine the impact of business cycles on business activities

Economic Systems

F.19 Explain the types of economic systems

F.20 Describe the relationship between government and business

F.21 Assess impact of government actions on business ventures

F.22 Explain the concept of private enterprise

F.23 Assess factors affecting a business's profit

F.24 Determine factors affecting business risk

F.25 Explain the concept of competition

F.26 Describe types of market structures

F.27 Determine the impact of small business/entrepreneurship on market economies

International Concepts

F.28 Explain the nature of international trade

F.29 Describe small-business opportunities in international trade

F.30 Determine the impact of cultural and social environments on world trade

F.31 Explain the impact of exchange rates on trade

F.32 Evaluate influences on a nation's ability to trade

[G] FINANCIAL LITERACY: Understands personal money-management concepts, procedures, and strategies

Money Basics

G.01 Explain forms of financial exchange (cash, credit, debit, etc.)

G.02 Describe functions of money (medium of exchange, unit of measure, store of value)

G.03 Describe the sources of income (wages/salaries, interest, rent, dividends, transfer payments, etc.)

G.04 Recognize types of currency (paper money, coins, banknotes, government bonds, treasury notes, etc.)

G.05 Read and interpret a pay stub

G.06 Explain the time value of money

G.07 Describe costs associated with credit

G.08 Explain legal responsibilities associated with use of money

G.09 Use money effectively

Financial Services

G.10 Describe services provided by financial institutions

G.11 Explain legal responsibilities of financial institutions

G.12 Explain costs associated with use of financial services

STARTINGUP NCSEE

Financial Services (continued)

G.13 Select financial institution

G.14 Open account with financial institution

Personal Money Management

G.15 Set financial goals

G.16 Develop savings plan

G.17 Develop spending plan

G.18 Make deposits to and withdrawals from account

G.19 Complete financial instruments

G.20 Maintain financial records

G.21 Read and reconcile financial statements

G.22 Correct errors with account

G.23 Explain types of investments

G.24 Invest money

G.25 Develop personal budget

G.26 Build positive credit history

G.27 Improve/repair creditworthiness

[H] PROFESSIONAL DEVELOPMENT: Understands concepts and strategies needed for career exploration, development, and growth

Career Planning

H.01 Evaluate career opportunities based on current/future economy

H.02 Analyze employer expectations in the business environment

H.03 Explain the rights of workers

H.04 Select and use sources of career information

H.05 Determine tentative occupational interest

H.06 Explain employment opportunities in entrepreneurship

Job-Seeking Skills

H.07 Utilize job-search strategies

H.08 Complete a job application

H.09 Interview for a job

H.10 Write a follow-up letter after job interviews

Job-Seeking Skills (continued)

H.11 Write a letter of application

H.12 Prepare a résumé

H.13 Describe techniques for obtaining work experience (e.g., volunteer activities, internships)

H.14 Explain the need for ongoing education as a worker

H.15 Explain possible advancement patterns for jobs

H.16 Determine skills needed to enhance career progression

H.17 Utilize resources that can contribute to professional development (e.g., trade journals/ periodicals, professional/trade associations, classes/seminars, trade shows, and mentors)

H.18 Use networking techniques for professional growth

Business Functions

The business activities performed by entrepreneurs in managing the business.

> **[I] FINANCIAL MANAGEMENT:** Understands the financial concepts and tools used in making business decisions

Accounting

I.01 Explain accounting standards (GAAP)

I.02 Prepare estimated/projected income statement

I.03 Estimate cash-flow needs

I.04 Prepare estimated/projected balance sheet

I.05 Calculate financial ratios

I.06 Determine and deposit payroll taxes

I.07 File tax returns

Finance

I.08 Explain the purposes and importance of obtaining business credit

I.09 Make critical decisions regarding acceptance of bank cards

I.10 Establish credit policies

I.11 Develop billing and collection policies

I.12 Describe use of credit bureaus

I.13 Explain the nature of overhead/operating expenses

I.14 Determine financing needed to start a business

I.15 Determine risks associated with obtaining business credit

I.16 Explain sources of financial assistance

STARTINGUP NCSEE

Finance (continued)

I.17 Explain loan evaluation criteria used by lending institutions

I.18 Select sources of business loans

I.19 Establish relationship with financial institutions

I.20 Complete loan application process

I.21 Determine business's value

Money Management

I.22 Establish financial goals and objectives

I.23 Develop and monitor budget

I.24 Manage cash flow

I.25 Explain the nature of capital investment

I.26 Foster a positive financial reputation

I.27 Implement procedures for managing debt

I.28 Supervise/implement regular accounting procedures and financial reports

[J] HUMAN RESOURCE MANAGEMENT: Understands the concepts, systems, and strategies needed to acquire, motivate, develop, and terminate staff

Organizing

J.01 Develop a personnel organizational plan

J.02 Develop job descriptions

J.03 Develop compensation plan/incentive systems

J.04 Organize work/projects for others

J.05 Delegate responsibility for job tasks

Staffing

J.06 Determine hiring needs

J.07 Recruit new employees

J.08 Screen job applications/résumés

J.09 Interview job applicants

J.10 Select new employees

J.11 Negotiate new hire's salary/pay

J.12 Dismiss/Fire employee

Training/Development

J.13 Orient new employees (management's role)
J.14 Conduct training class/program
J.15 Coach employees

Morale/Motivation

J.16 Exhibit leadership skills
J.17 Encourage team building
J.18 Recognize/reward employees
J.19 Handle employee complaints/grievances
J.20 Ensure equitable opportunities for employees
J.21 Build organizational culture

Assessment

J.22 Assess employee morale
J.23 Provide feedback on work efforts
J.24 Assess employee performance
J.25 Take remedial action with employee
J.26 Conduct exit interviews

[K] INFORMATION MANAGEMENT: Understands the concepts, systems, and tools needed to access, process, maintain, evaluate, and disseminate information for business decision-making

Record Keeping

K.01 Explain the nature of business records
K.02 Maintain record of daily financial transactions
K.03 Record and report sales tax
K.04 Develop payroll record keeping system
K.05 Maintain personnel records
K.06 Maintain customer records

Technology

K.07 Explain ways that technology impacts business
K.08 Use Personal Information Management/Productivity applications
K.09 Demonstrate writing/publishing applications
K.10 Demonstrate presentation applications
K.11 Demonstrate database applications

Technology (continued)

K.12 Demonstrate spreadsheet applications

K.13 Demonstrate collaborative/groupware applications

K.14 Determine venture's technology needs

Information Acquisition

K.15 Select sources of business start-up information

K.16 Conduct an environmental scan to obtain marketing information

K.17 Monitor internal records for marketing information

K.18 Determine underlying customer needs/frustrations

[L] MARKETING MANAGEMENT: Understands the concepts, processes, and systems needed to determine and satisfy customer needs/wants/expectations, meet business goals/objectives, and create new product/service ideas

Product/Service Creation

L.01 Explain methods to generate a product/service idea

L.02 Generate product/service ideas

L.03 Assess opportunities for import substitution

L.04 Determine product/service to fill customer need

L.05 Determine initial feasibility of product/service ideas

L.06 Plan product/service mix

L.07 Choose product name

L.08 Determine unique selling proposition

L.09 Develop strategies to position product/service

L.10 Build brand/image

L.11 Evaluate customer experience

Marketing-information Management

L.12 Explain the concept of market and market identification

L.13 Describe the role of situation analysis in the marketing-planning process

L.14 Determine market segments

L.15 Select target markets

L.16 Conduct market analysis

Marketing-information Management (continued)

L.17 Explain the concept of marketing strategies

L.18 Describe the nature of marketing planning

L.19 Set a marketing budget

L.20 Develop marketing plan

L.21 Monitor and evaluate performance of marketing plan

Promotion

L.22 Describe the elements of the promotional mix

L.23 Calculate advertising media costs

L.24 Select advertising media

L.25 Prepare a promotional budget

L.26 Develop promotional plan for a business

L.27 Write a news release

L.28 Obtain publicity

L.29 Select sales-promotion options

L.30 Write sales letters

L.31 Manage online (www) activities

L.32 Evaluate effectiveness of advertising

Pricing

L.33 Calculate breakeven point

L.34 Explain factors affecting pricing decisions

L.35 Establish pricing objectives

L.36 Select pricing strategies

L.37 Set prices

L.38 Adjust prices to maximize profitability

Selling

L.39 Acquire product information for use in selling

L.40 Analyze product information to identify product features and benefits

L.41 Prepare for the sales presentation

L.42 Establish relationship with client/customer

L.43 Determine customer/client needs

L.44 Determine customer's buying motives for use in selling

L.45 Differentiate between consumer and organizational buying behavior

L.46 Recommend specific product

L.47 Convert customer/client objections into selling points

L.48 Close the sale

Selling (continued)

L.49 Demonstrate suggestion selling

L.50 Plan follow-up strategies for use in selling

L.51 Process sales documentation

L.52 Prospect for customers

L.53 Plan strategies for meeting sales quotas

L.54 Analyze sales reports

L.55 Train staff to support sales efforts

L.56 Analyze technology for use in the sales function

L.57 Manage online sales process

[M] OPERATIONS MANAGEMENT: Understands the processes and systems implemented to facilitate daily business operations.

Business Systems

M.01 Plan business layout

M.02 Determine equipment needs

M.03 Document business systems and procedures

M.04 Establish operating procedures

M.05 Develop project plans

M.06 Analyze business processes and procedures

M.07 Implement quality improvement techniques

M.08 Evaluate productivity of resources

M.09 Manage computer-based operating systems

Channel Management

M.10 Select business location

M.11 Select distribution channels

M.12 Develop and implement order-fulfillment processes

Purchasing/Procurement

M.13 Explain the buying process

M.14 Describe the nature of buyer reputation and vendor relationships

M.15 Establish company buying/purchasing policies

M.16 Conduct vendor search

Purchasing/Procurement

M.17 Choose vendors

M.18 Negotiate contracts with vendors

M.19 Place orders

M.20 Barter with vendors

Daily Operations

M.21 Schedule staff

M.22 Maintain inventory of products/supplies

M.23 Organize shipping/receiving

[N] RISK MANAGEMENT: Understands the concepts, strategies, and systems that businesses implement and enforce to minimize loss

Business Risks

N.01 Describe types of business risk

N.02 Determine ways that small businesses protect themselves against loss

N.03 Establish controls to prevent embezzlement/theft

N.04 Establish and implement systems to protect customer/employee confidentiality

N.05 Determine business's liabilities

N.06 Explain ways to transfer risk

N.07 Obtain insurance coverage

N.08 Develop strategies to protect computer (digital) data

N.09 Develop security policies and procedures

N.10 Establish safety policies and procedures

N.11 Protect assets from creditors

N.12 Establish parameters for staff responsibility/authority

N.13 Develop continuation plan

Legal Considerations

N.14 Explain legal issues affecting businesses

N.15 Protect intellectual property rights

N.16 Select form of business ownership

N.17 Obtain legal documents for business operations

N.18 Describe the nature of businesses' reporting requirements

N.19 Adhere to personnel regulations

N.20 Implement workplace regulations (including OSHA, ADA)

N.21 Develop strategies for legal/government compliance

► THE**NATIONAL CONTENT STANDARDS**
FOR ENTREPRENEURSHIP EDUCATION

[O] STRATEGIC MANAGEMENT: Understands the processes, strategies, and systems needed to guide the overall business organization

Planning

O.01 Conduct S.W.O.T.S. analysis
O.02 Conduct competitive analysis
O.03 Evaluate business acquisition options
O.04 Develop company goals/objectives
O.05 Develop business mission
O.06 Forecast income/sales
O.07 Conduct break-even analysis
O.08 Develop action plans
O.09 Develop business plan

Controlling

O.10 Use budgets to control operations
O.11 Develop expense-control plans
O.12 Analyze cash-flow patterns
O.13 Interpret financial statements
O.14 Analyze operating results in relation to budget/industry
O.15 Track performance of business plan

STARTINGUP NOW

Before you begin, take a moment to familiarize yourself with the StartingUp Now structure. Each StartingUp Now lesson is divided into two sections. The first part, the StartingUp Plan, strategically outlines how each StartingUp Key lesson should be presented in the classroom. The second part, the StartingUp Key, will be used to define and demonstrate each business concept and how they work within the scope of good business practices. We invite you to look over the next few pages to help you navigate through your StartingUp Now experience.

STARTINGUP PLAN GUIDE [Part1]

Below is the detail of elements found in each StartingUp Plan. Adhere to the NCSEE standards listed on each page to help guide you though the architecture of each lesson.

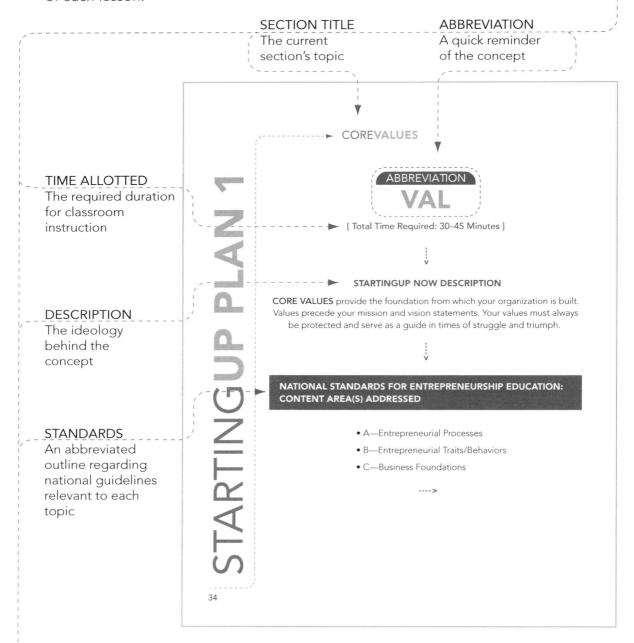

SECTION TITLE
The current section's topic

ABBREVIATION
A quick reminder of the concept

TIME ALLOTTED
The required duration for classroom instruction

DESCRIPTION
The ideology behind the concept

STANDARDS
An abbreviated outline regarding national guidelines relevant to each topic

STARTINGUP PLAN 1

CORE VALUES

ABBREVIATION
VAL

[Total Time Required: 30–45 Minutes]

STARTINGUP NOW DESCRIPTION

CORE VALUES provide the foundation from which your organization is built. Values precede your mission and vision statements. Your values must always be protected and serve as a guide in times of struggle and triumph.

NATIONAL STANDARDS FOR ENTREPRENEURSHIP EDUCATION: CONTENT AREA(S) ADDRESSED

• A—Entrepreneurial Processes
• B—Entrepreneurial Traits/Behaviors
• C—Business Foundations

---->

34

STARTINGUP PLAN GUIDE [Part2] ◂-----------

This page details each StartingUp Key's desired goal for you and your students. Be sure to utilize the StartingUp Skill Center (SUSC) whenever possible.

Learning Objectives ---->

- Students will define *value*.
- Students will correlate why values are important in business.
- Students will list how values are needed to *guide* an organization.
- Students will identify values that will guide their businesses.

Performance Objectives ---->

- **Model** ----> Review the values and their descriptions listed by Don Soderquist.
- **Activity** ----> Students will identify three core values and examine:
  - ----> How will these values reflect on who they are?
  - ----> How will these values impact the way they treat others?
  - ----> How will these values impact the way they operate their businesses?
- **SU Plan** ----> Students must select ONLY one of their core values identified as the most important one and add it to their plans.

StartingUp Skill Center Application ---->

- Students research values of other companies, persons, and businesses on the SUSC or via the Internet. Students will identify their core values and save them as part of their business plans online.

Materials Needed ---->

StartingUp Now Book, computer, Internet access, paper, pen/pencil

35

OBJECTIVES
The intended path for each lesson

APPLICATION
Indicates SUSC interaction for students

STEPS
Details items needed to instruct

STARTINGUP KEY GUIDE

Use the StartingUp Key to maneuver through each business concept presented. Create an interactive environment for your students with hands-on exercises relevant to each topic explored.

SECTION TITLE
The current section's topic

ABBREVIATION
A quick reminder of the concept

DESCRIPTION
The ideology behind the concept

MODELS
An example illustrating the current concept

STEPS
Exercises that implement the concept into the business plan

KEEP IT GOING
Helpful tips and tools to further the understanding of the concept

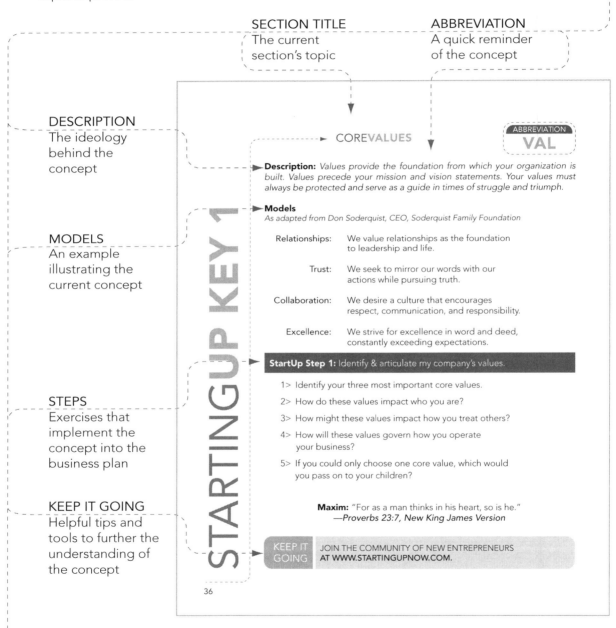

CORE**VALUES**

ABBREVIATION
VAL

Description: *Values provide the foundation from which your organization is built. Values precede your mission and vision statements. Your values must always be protected and serve as a guide in times of struggle and triumph.*

Models
As adapted from Don Soderquist, CEO, Soderquist Family Foundation

Relationships: We value relationships as the foundation to leadership and life.

Trust: We seek to mirror our words with our actions while pursuing truth.

Collaboration: We desire a culture that encourages respect, communication, and responsibility.

Excellence: We strive for excellence in word and deed, constantly exceeding expectations.

StartUp Step 1: Identify & articulate my company's values.

1> Identify your three most important core values.

2> How do these values impact who you are?

3> How might these values impact how you treat others?

4> How will these values govern how you operate your business?

5> If you could only choose one core value, which would you pass on to your children?

Maxim: "For as a man thinks in his heart, so is he."
—*Proverbs 23:7, New King James Version*

KEEP IT GOING   JOIN THE COMMUNITY OF NEW ENTREPRENEURS AT WWW.STARTINGUPNOW.COM.

STARTINGUP KEY 1

36

► FOREWORD

Entrepreneurship is what has driven the free enterprise system in our country since our founding fathers established the foundation for our way of life. Brian Jenkins is an entrepreneur by heart and by experience. I have known him for almost 10 years. During that time I have been impressed with his passion for entrepreneurship. I have witnessed his ability to create and build his own business based on a clear understanding of what it takes to start a business founded on vision, mission, and values with limited resources. His ability to "stick with it" in difficult circumstances and maintain his commitment is precisely the type of leadership entrepreneurs and business owners need to see in today's economically challenged marketplace.

Brian has demonstrated a passion for training youth, educators, business owners, and the formerly incarcerated in free market principles. I believe that Brian has the personal experience, integrity, training skills, and know-how to impact business owners for years to come.

When ambitious individuals have an idea that they believe has merit as a product or service, it is difficult to find a road map that helps them get started and carry through to completion. Brian has framed StartingUp Now in such a way that it provides a time-tested, step-by-step process to achieve success. I believe that StartingUp Now will have a significant impact on all who read it.

—Donald G. Soderquist, ret.,
Vice Chairman and Chief Operating Officer
Walmart Stores, Inc.

► INTRODUCTION

StartingUp Now is a practical, easy-to-understand business-planning guide for the new entrepreneur with great ideas and limited business planning knowledge, who needs steps to get started. *StartingUp Now* employs elements of today's texting culture to quickly communicate essential business principles. Each *StartingUp Key* leads the future entrepreneur through a memorable abbreviation, informative definition, useful examples, and constructive prompts in a journal-style format that ultimately provides users with the opportunity to formulate their business plans.

Upon formulating your plan with the StartingUp Business Plan Template, log in to your customized profile page on the StartingUp Now Skill Center (SUSC) and enter your business plan information on the online template. For those with mobile devices, you can access your business plan and other tools and resources on the go.

Welcome to *StartingUp Now!*

CORE**VALUES**

ABBREVIATION
VAL

[Total Time Required: 30–45 Minutes]

STARTINGUP NOW DESCRIPTION

CORE VALUES provide the foundation from which your organization is built. Values precede your mission and vision statements. Your values must always be protected and serve as a guide in times of struggle and triumph.

NATIONAL STANDARDS FOR ENTREPRENEURSHIP EDUCATION: CONTENT AREA(S) ADDRESSED

- A—Entrepreneurial Processes
- B—Entrepreneurial Traits/Behaviors
- C—Business Foundations

---->

Learning Objectives ---->

- Students will define *value*.
- Students will correlate why values are important in business.
- Students will list how values are needed to *guide* an organization.
- Students will identify values that will guide their businesses.

Performance Objectives ---->

- **Model** ----> Review the values and their descriptions listed by Don Soderquist.
- **Activity** ----> Students will identify three core values and examine:
  - ----> How will these values reflect on who they are?
  - ----> How will these values impact the way they treat others?
  - ----> How will these values impact the way they operate their businesses?
- **SU Plan** ----> Students must select ONLY one of their core values identified as the most important one and add it to their plans.

StartingUp Skill Center Application ---->

- Students research values of other companies, persons, and businesses on the SUSC or via the Internet. Students will identify their core values and save them as part of their business plans online.

Materials Needed ---->

StartingUp Now Book, computer, Internet access, paper, pen/pencil

ABBREVIATION
VAL

Description: *Values provide the foundation from which your organization is built. Values precede your mission and vision statements. Your values must always be protected and serve as a guide in times of struggle and triumph.*

Models
As adapted from Don Soderquist, CEO, Soderquist Family Foundation

Relationships:	We value relationships as the foundation to leadership and life.
Trust:	We seek to mirror our words with our actions while pursuing truth.
Collaboration:	We desire a culture that encourages respect, communication, and responsibility.
Excellence:	We strive for excellence in word and deed, constantly exceeding expectations.

StartUp Step 1: Identify & articulate my company's values.

1> Identify your three most important core values.

2> How do these values impact who you are?

3> How might these values impact how you treat others?

4> How will these values govern how you operate your business?

5> If you could only choose one core value, which would you pass on to your children?

Maxim: "For as a man thinks in his heart, so is he."
—*Proverbs 23:7, New King James Version*

KEEP IT GOING JOIN THE COMMUNITY OF NEW ENTREPRENEURS AT WWW.STARTINGUPNOW.COM.

STARTINGUP KEY 1

MISSION**STATEMENT**

ABBREVIATION
MST

[Total Time Required: 30–45 Minutes]

STARTINGUP NOW DESCRIPTION

The **MISSION STATEMENT** provides the purpose for the operation of the business. It defines what you want the business to become—not necessarily its current status. The Mission Statement should be challenging but achievable.

NATIONAL STANDARDS FOR ENTREPRENEURSHIP EDUCATION: CONTENT AREA(S) ADDRESSED

- A—Entrepreneurial Processes
- B—Entrepreneurial Traits/Behaviors

---->

- Students will gain an understanding of the MST.

- Students will identify the purpose of their companies' existence.

- Students will write an MST for their new businesses.

Performance Objectives ---->

- **Model** ----> Review and reflect on the mission statements of the model companies and identify their purposes.
  ----> Reflect on Charles Perkhurt's statement from the Maxim: "Purpose is what gives life meaning."
  ----> Students will research other companies and identify their purposes in the marketplace.

- **Activity** ----> Students should identify the purpose of their companies.
  ----> Students should state what they hope the company will accomplish.

- **SU Plan** ----> Students should establish their Mission Statements and write them out in their templates.
  ----> Students should memorize their Mission Statements.

StartingUp Skill Center Application ---->

- Research Mission Statements created by other companies. Once the students have created their own Mission Statements, they can add them to their business plans to save and access online.

Materials Needed ---->

Computers, Internet access, pens, paper

► MISSIONSTATEMENT

ABBREVIATION
MST

Description: *The MST provides purpose. It defines what you want the business to become—not necessarily its current status. The MST should be challenging but also achievable.*

Models

"To equip youth workers with the expertise necessary to train young people to be skillful entrepreneurs with integrity."

—Entrenuity, NFP

"Our mission revolves around one word: patience. In earnest pursuit of excellent performance and outstanding client service, **patience** is our over-arching virtue. By taking a long-term view, we are able to build our firm around these core values: focus, independent thinking, and teamwork."

—Ariel Capital Investments, Inc.

StartUp Step 2: Establish my company's MST.

1> Why am I starting the business? What are the motivating factors?

2> What is the company's purpose?

3> What do I hope the company will accomplish?

4> What product does my company sell or what service does it provide?

5> How is my company different?

Maxim: "Purpose is what gives life meaning."
—*Charles H. Perkhurst*

KEEP IT GOING
GET ON-GOING SUPPORT FOR YOUR NEW VENTURE AT WWW.STARTINGUPNOW.COM.

VISIONSTATEMENT

ABBREVIATION

VIS

[Total Time Required: 30 Minutes]

STARTINGUP NOW DESCRIPTION

The VISION STATEMENT is the idealistic objective that stretches an organization beyond its current status and declares its future purpose. It is the level of excellence or accomplishment that the business is motivated to achieve. The VIS represents the "best" or "ideal."

NATIONAL STANDARDS FOR ENTREPRENEURSHIP EDUCATION: CONTENT AREA(S) ADDRESSED

- A—Entrepreneurial Processes
- B—Entrepreneurial Traits/Behaviors
- C—Business Foundations

- Within the context of their businesses, students will identify the ideal scenario if their businesses realized there fullest potentials and accomplishments.

- Students will learn how to develop/create a VIS.
  - ----> It is VERY IMPORTANT for students to be able to dream of the possibilities without hindrance.
  - ----> It is necessary for students to see the possibilities of the business potential in an ideal environment.

- **Model** ----> Review the model Vision Statements. Identify the "grandiose" vision in each of the companies. List out how the vision stretches each of the companies.

- **Activity** ----> Complete steps 1–4 in StartUp Step 3.
  - ----> The Vision Statement must be reduced to three sentences or fewer.
  - ----> Students should be able to state their vision statements in less than 30 seconds.

- **SU Plan** ----> Students will write out their Vision Statements in their templates.

- Research and review vision statements from resources on the SUSC. Highlight vision statements that might be helpful to the SUSC community and share it with those in your network.

- Write and save your Vision Statement to the StartingUp Now Online Business Plan.

StartingUp Now book, computer, Internet access, paper, pen/pencil

VISION**STATEMENT**

ABBREVIATION
VIS

Description: *The VIS is the idealistic objective that stretches an organization beyond its current status and declares its future purpose. It is the level of excellence or accomplishment that the business is motivated to achieve. The VIS represents the "best."*

Models

"To see young people around the globe receive hands-on entrepreneurship training that develops skills and values to be leaders in their chosen marketplace, community, and family."

—Entrenuity, NFP

"To bring inspiration and innovation to every athlete in the world."

—Nike

"McDonald's vision is to be the world's best quick service restaurant experience. Being the best means providing outstanding quality, service, cleanliness, and value, so that we make every customer in every restaurant smile."

—McDonald's, Inc.

StartUp Step 3: To cast a vision for your business, let's start by doing the following:

1> Five years from now your business is receiving the Small Business of the Year Award. In what categories would the business receive nominations (leadership, green technology, innovation, etc.)?

2> What are the accomplished goals that you can look back on?

3> What impact has your business made on your community or industry?

4> What do you want to be known for?

Next, condense your findings from each of the four numbered sections into a single sentence statement.

KEEP IT GOING FOR HELP TO MAKE YOUR VISION A REALITY, LOG ON TO **WWW.STARTINGUPNOW.COM.**

Now, take the sentences and reduce them to a short statement that you can almost memorize.

If your statement totals three sentences or fewer, you're done! If not, summarize your statement into three sentences or fewer and verbally share it with someone in 30 seconds or fewer. If it takes longer, you have more work to do!

Maxim: "Desire is the starting point of all achievement, not a hope, not a wish, but a keen pulsating desire which transcends everything."
—*Napoleon Hill*

MYVIS ◄- -

STARTINGUP PLAN 4

ABBREVIATION
EXE

[Total Time Required: 45 Minutes]

STARTINGUP NOW DESCRIPTION

The **EXECUTIVE SUMMARY** describes the company, the product/service being sold, and the uniqueness of the investment opportunity. Potential financiers will focus FIRST on the EXE; based on this, they will then decide whether or not to examine the viability of the business for investment.

NATIONAL STANDARDS FOR ENTREPRENEURSHIP EDUCATION: CONTENT AREA(S) ADDRESSED

- A—Entrepreneurial Processes
- C—Business Foundations
- I—Financial Management

- Students will gain an understanding of the EXE and realize its importance in their own business plans.
  - ----> The EXE is a significant first-read document of the business plan.
  - ----> The EXE is typically succinct and outlines the opportunity for an investor.
  - ----> Based on the opportunity presented in the EXE, an investor will determine if they will read the business plan in its entirety.
  - ----> It should be noted that the EXE will often change or be edited multiple times as new information is gained during the research process.

Performance Objectives --->

- **Model** ----> Discuss the concepts of products and services.

- **Activity** ----> Students must identify the products/services they are selling and list its features and benefits.
  - ----> Students must identify the investment opportunities their businesses present for an investment—possibly providing snapshot data of the financial opportunity.

- **SU Plan** ----> Students will write out their EXEs in their templates and on their business plans on the SUSC.

StartingUp Skill Center Application --->

- Students will research Executive Summaries of other businesses and entrepreneurs via the SUSC within the same industry (i.e., restaurant, hair care, tech). Note the products/services that distinguishes the businesses from each other in the same industry.

- Students will write and save their EXEs. As noted, they will likely change the EXE several times as new information is gained through the business planning/ research process.

Materials Needed --->

StartingUp Now Book, computer, Internet access, paper, pen/pencil

STARTINGUP KEY 4

Description: *The EXE describes the company, the product/service being sold, and the uniqueness of the investment opportunity. Potential financiers will focus first on the EXE; based on this, they will then decide whether or not to examine the viability of the business for investment.*

Models

Pet Daycare Executive Summary:

Pet Daycare offers on-site pet-sitting services for dogs and cats, providing the personal loving pet care that the owners themselves would provide if they were there. While there are currently eight businesses offering pet-sitting in Oak Park, only four of these offer on-site pet care and none offers "pet visit" services for working pet owners. Based on the size of our market and our defined market area, our sales projections for the first year are $340,000. We are seeking an operating line of $150,000 to finance our first year growth. Together, the co-owners have invested $62,000 to meet working capital requirements.

Wendy's Franchise Executive Summary:

Wendy's International, Inc., and its subsidiaries engage in the operation, development, and franchising of a range of quick service, casual restaurants. Wendy's International, Inc., is one of the world's largest restaurant operating and franchising companies with $11.6 billion in system-wide sales and more than 9,700 total restaurants. The company's quality brands are Wendy's Old Fashioned Hamburgers, Tim Hortons, and Baja Fresh Mexican Grill. The company invested in two additional quality brands during 2002: Cafe Express and Pasta Pomodoro. Wendy's International, Inc., was founded in 1969 by Dave Thomas and is based in Dublin, Ohio. This offering represents an excellent opportunity for an investor to purchase an absolute triple net leased, free-standing Wendy's with an outstanding operator of 20 Wendy's restaurants in Chicago, who is consistently in the top 10% operators in the nation. This approximately 3,000+/- square-foot, freestanding Wendy's property generates $136,000 annually, and is on a brand-new 20-year absolute lease, with 10% rental escalations every fifth year.

KEEP IT GOING | JOIN THE COMMUNITY OF NEW ENTREPRENEURS AT WWW.STARTINGUPNOW.COM.

1> Describe the product or service you are selling.

2> List out the unique features and describe how they directly benefit the customer.

3> What makes this investment opportunity unique?

Maxim: "Give me six hours to chop down a tree and I'll
spend the first hour sharpening the ax."
—*Abraham Lincoln, 16th President of the United States of America.*

MYEXE ◄- -

ELEVATOR**SPEECH**

ABBREVIATION
ESP

[Total Time Required: 30–40 Minutes]

v

STARTINGUP NOW DESCRIPTION

A brief yet persuasive description of what you do, the product you produce, and the service you provide. The **ESP** will summarize your business in the time it might take an elevator to go from the ground floor to the penthouse.

v

NATIONAL STANDARDS FOR ENTREPRENEURSHIP EDUCATION: CONTENT AREA(S) ADDRESSED

- A—Entrepreneurial Processes
- B—Entrepreneurial Traits/Behaviors
- C—Business Foundations
- H—Professional Development

---->

Learning Objectives ---->

- Students will create a mini ESP that:
  ----> is one minute in presentation
  ----> is CLEAR and to the POINT—you don't have much time
  ----> will identify who they are and their roles in the companies
- Students will verbally discuss the products they sell or service
  they provide, typically highlighting 1–2 aspect of their businesses

Performance Objectives ---->

- **Model** ----> Explain the ESP. It should be easy to understand.
  ----> The ESP must be brief, precise, and to the point. There
  should be no lengthy pauses that consume needed time.
  ----> Make sure all the questions are answered: your name,
  your product, and the service you provide.
- **Activity** ----> Participants should write out their ESPs on a 3 x 5 note card
  and practice with a friend.
  ----> Participants should be able to complete their ESPs in 1 minute or less.
- **SU Plan** ----> Participants should practice their ESPs multiple times throughout
  the duration of the class.

StartingUp Skill Center Application ---->

Look up various ESPs on the SUSC. Observe the various styles
and identify tips to help improve your ESP.

Materials Needed ---->

StartingUp Now Book, computer, Internet access, paper, pen/pencil, 3 x 5 note card

► ELEVATOR**SPEECH**

ABBREVIATION
ESP

Description: *A brief yet persuasive description of what you do, the product you produce, and the service you provide. The ESP will summarize your business expertise in the time it might take for an elevator to journey from the ground floor to the penthouse.*

Models

"I turn conflict into agreement. I'm Robbie Smith of the Business Conflict Resolution Center. My workshops and coaching reduce your conflict. We teach people how to understand, discuss, and resolve conflict so they can live happier lives. Let US replace the conflict in your life."

—*Business Conflict Resolution Center, LLC*

"Hello, I teach college graduates manners and business etiquette for interviews. Politeness promotes profits in the interview process. I'm Jasmine Jones, and it's my pleasure to meet you!"

"I'm Walter Smith of Romantic Meals. I specialize in providing immaculate 5-star meals for anniversaries, birthdays, or special occasions at your home. We provide the meal so you can provide the mood!"

—*Romantic Meals, LLC*

StartUp Step 5: Your ESP should be very clear, descriptive, and to the point.

Tips for your ESP:

1> Make it easy to understand.

2> Make it brief, precise, and to the point.

3> Leave no questions that need to be answered.

4> Practice it verbally. Try to say your ESP in 60 seconds or less.

Maxim: KIS Method—Keep It Simple

KEEP IT GOING SHARPEN YOUR ENTREPRENEURIAL SKILLS AT WWW.STARTINGUPNOW.COM.

BIO**GRAPHY**

ABBREVIATION
BIO

[Total Time Required: 45 Minutes]

STARTINGUP NOW DESCRIPTION

Everyone has a story. Tell yours. Your BIO is the personal
story of how you got started, your motivation, your skills,
and your goals. Make this personal—make it your own..

NATIONAL STANDARDS FOR ENTREPRENEURSHIP EDUCATION: CONTENT AREA(S) ADDRESSED

- A—Entrepreneurial Processes
- B—Entrepreneurial Traits/Behaviors
- H—Professional Development

STARTINGUP PLAN 6

- Students will learn to tell the personal side of how their businesses came into being. It's necessary to understand how their backgrounds or personal circumstances helped shape them. This is a key tool in developing their goals and objectives, both personal and corporate, for their business planning.

- Students will tweak their BIOs after the business plan is complete. Expect many edits, and it will likely change overtime as the students grow in their experiences.

Performance Objectives ---->

- **Model** ----> Lead a discussion to help students identify where they are from (i.e., school, neighborhood, organization).

- **Activity** ----> Students should complete a written response beginning with, "My Journey began when…" for example. Students should refer to a specific incident that serves as a starting point.
  ----> Identify a time frame or approximate date when the "incident" took place to spark your idea. This will serve as a point of reference.
  ----> Why do I continue? I believe it's for the reason of…" Students should list out 2–3 reasons on how they have persevered through that circumstance. This circumstance often will be very personal and sometimes emotional as people share their life stories.

- **SU Plan** ----> Students will write their BIOs in the template and on their StartingUp Business Plan Templates on the SUSC.

StartingUp Skill Center Application ---->

Look up the BIOs of entrepreneurs on the SUSC. Identify the motivating factors that shaped their entrepreneurial odysseys. Identify any related correlations, interests and personal commonalities with which your students can identify.

Materials Needed ---->

StartingUp Now Book, computer, Internet access, paper, pen/pencil, poster-sized paper

► BIOGRAPHY

ABBREVIATION
BIO

Description: *Everyone has a story. Tell yours. Your BIO is the personal story of how you got started, your motivation, your skills, and your goals. Make this personal.*

Model

"In the sixth grade my parents forced me to attend an entrepreneurship program at my school. My friend and I were the youngest in the class. I was nervous, scared, and really wanted to play on the basketball team instead of being in the class. The class taught us a lot about business. We identified a market need (vending), created a business plan, and opened for business. The business was very prosperous over the next two years. We made over $10,000 annually. We were introduced to investing and wanted to grow to the next phase. Upon going to high school, I started additional businesses and was fascinated by the stock market and wanted to learn more. I completed a 2-year internship program with a large investment firm in New York, and now I'm a First Year Investor with that same investment firm in NYC. It all started with that entrepreneurship class; it taught me 'anything is possible.'"

—*Stephan Hall, First Year Investor, Goldman Sachs*

StartUp Step 6: Writing your personal story can be both challenging and revealing. Let the following questions prompt you. Go ahead…get started.

THIS IS YOUR STORY

1> My name is _____ and I'm from _____.

2> My journey started when…

3> This happened in _____ (year) of when I was _____.

4> Why do I continue? I believe it's for the reason of _____.

5> My words of wisdom are…

Maxim: "What would you attempt to do if you knew you would not fail?"
—*Author Unknown*

KEEP IT
GOING
FIND BIO EXAMPLES FROM OTHER ENTREPRENEURS
AT WWW.STARTINGUPNOW.COM.

THE**BIG IDEA**

[Total Time Required: 30–40 Minutes]

STARTINGUP NOW DESCRIPTION

Coming up with a great business idea doesn't need to be complicated. Combine a NEED with something you love to do, and then create YOUR business.

NATIONAL STANDARDS FOR ENTREPRENEURSHIP EDUCATION: CONTENT AREA(S) ADDRESSED

- A—Entrepreneurial Processes
- B—Entrepreneurial Traits/Behaviors
- C—Business Foundations
- L—Marketing Management
- H—Professional Development

---->

- Students will identify their IDEAs they have for a business. This is often deemed as a freethinking "IDEATION" activity in which they come up with various ideas based on their interests and hobbies that can then be turned into a business opportunity.

  Technically, there are no bad IDEA's. It must be noted, however, that the IDEA should be respectful and not promote negative or harmful behaviors.

- **Model** ----> Discuss various hobbies/interests and have students select which of these for which they would like to get paid.
  ----> Narrow the list to their top three choices. Rank their lists in order of preference from their top (1) to the lowest (3).

- **Activity** ----> Have students list how their IDEA meets a specific need. Is that need being fulfilled? If so, list out who is currently filling the need?
  ----> Students should then list out at least 3 steps in which the idea can be improved.
  ----> Students should then list specific ways in which they can make the IDEA uniquely theirs.

- **SU Plan** ----> Students will write out their IDEAs in their templates and/or in their online business plans on the SUSC.

Research various operational businesses and identify the specific marketplace need being met. Analyze the businesses identified using the same methodology from the Performance Objectives. This process will help in narrowing marketplace needs that the students' businesses can meet—the narrower the focus the easier to manage/evaluate.

StartingUp Now Book, computer, Internet access, paper, pen/pencil

► THE**BIG IDEA**

ABBREVIATION
IDEA

Description: *Coming up with a great business idea doesn't need to be complicated. Combine a NEED with something you love to do, and then create your business.*

Models

"People enjoy eating ice cream, so why shouldn't dogs enjoy ice cream, too? Sounds crazy to some, but the lack of frozen treats for my dogs gave me this bright and unique idea."

—*Chellsy Charles, Owner, Chilly-Dawgs*

"Store brands of lotions irritate my skin. After trying prescriptions from doctors and home remedies, I learned how to make my own lotion using natural products. Now I sell it for others just like me."

—*Kim Porter, Founder, LeNae Natural Lotions*

"My grandmother is especially important to me and she still enjoys looking her best. Although she lacks the mobility she used to have, she still enjoys her day at the spa. I now provide home-based facials, manicures, and pedicures for seniors at their homes."

—*Julia Smiley, CEO, Mobile Spas, LLC.*

StartUp Step 7: Generating Ideas

Businesses typically invent a new product or service to fulfill a need or improve an existing product or service already in the marketplace. Oftentimes entrepreneurs will center their interests, experiences, passions, and skill sets toward their business ideas. To put it simply, Do What You Love.

1> Make a list of your hobbies, interests, or talents. Which of these would you do whether you got paid for it or not?

2> Narrow this list to your top three choices.

3> Which of these things could satisfy a marketplace need? Is that need currently being met? If so, how and by whom? Can it be improved?

4> How can you make this idea uniquely yours?

KEEP IT
GOING
SHARE YOUR BUSINESS IDEAS AND EXPLORE OTHERS
AT WWW.STARTINGUPNOW.COM.

Maxim: "Find a job you love and you'll never work a day in your life."
—*Confucius*

MY**IDEA** ◄--

STARTINGUP PLAN 8

ABBREVIATION
LEG

[Total Time Required: 30–40 Minutes]

STARTINGUP NOW DESCRIPTION

Legal structures are designed for the protection of the business owner and its customers. There are several types of legal structures. The legal structure best suited for your business should be defined by your personal and business needs.

NATIONAL STANDARDS FOR ENTREPRENEURSHIP EDUCATION: CONTENT AREA(S) ADDRESSED

- B—Entrepreneurial Traits/Behaviors
- C—Business Foundations
- F—Economics

- Students will gain an understanding of the various types of legal structures used most often by new business owners. LEGs can be complex depending on the needs and goals of the business.

- Students will develop an understanding of the importance of consulting a legal expert, such as an attorney, who can help match the appropriate LEG with the needs of the business owner.

Performance Objectives ---->

- **Model** ----> Review legal structures as presented in the StartingUp Book.

- **Activity** ----> Students will begin to outline the legal structure of their companies.
  ----> Students will list the owner(s) of their businesses by name.
  ----> Students must consider their capital needs to get the business started. The capital source of their businesses—loans vs. selling a portion of the business—will have a direct impact on the legal structure selected.
  ----> Student owner(s) must determine if they plan to grow, sell, or expand the business over the next few years. This also has a direct impact on the type of legal structure selected.
  ----> Students will review and select which legal structure provides the most protection for their personal assets.
  ----> Students will identify their legal advisors/attorneys by name.

- **SU Plan** ----> Students will list the legal structure selected in their templates, provide bullet points explaining why this particular legal structure was selected, and identify their legal advisors/attorneys by name.

StartingUp Skill Center Application ---->

Research additional detailed information concerning legal structures, licenses, permits, and other compliance regulations needed for your business. You may also research and identify a legal expert from the SUSC network.

Materials Needed ---->

StartingUp Now Book, computer, Internet access, paper, pen/pencil

STARTINGUP KEY 8

Description: *Legal structures are designed for the protection of the business owner and its customers. There are several types of legal structures, and which one is best depends on your personal and business needs.*

Models

Most entrepreneurs select one of the following legal structures for their businesses. While you should educate yourself by conducting your own research, it is also wise to consult an attorney or legal expert to review your selection and confirm that you've chosen the legal structure that will best serve your business now and in the future.

Sole Proprietorship means one owner who assumes all risk and receives all the rewards. Typically, they are less expensive to form and operate.

Partnerships are a legal structure in which the partners (owners) share the profits and losses of the business. Partnerships are generally not taxed on profits prior to the profits being distributed to the owners.

Limited Liability Corporations (LLC) is a flexible legal structure that blends aspects of both a partnership and corporation. The primary characteristic an LLC shares with a corporation is limited liability, and the primary characteristic it shares with a partnership is the availability of pass-through income taxation. It is often more flexible than a corporation and well suited for companies with a single owner.

C Corporations can have an unlimited number of owners. They are publicly traded, meaning individuals, other corporations, partnerships, and the general public can purchase shares of stock in the company. A key distinction of a C Corp. is that the income is generally taxed. Large companies generally (Nike, Dell, Apple, etc.) are C Corporations.

StartUp Step 8: Answer the following questions to help select a legal structure:

1> Will you be the only owner of the business or will there be shared ownership?

KEEP IT GOING LEARN MORE ABOUT ESTABLISHING LEGAL STRUCTURES AND OTHER OPERATIONAL DETAILS **AT WWW.STARTINGUPNOW.COM.**

2> Do you plan to start the business with your own money? Will you secure a loan? Should you consider selling a portion of the business in exchange for investment capital?

3> Do you plan to grow, expand, or sell the business in the first 1–3 years?

4> Should you be concerned with protecting your personal assets (home, savings, automobiles, etc.) in the event that you are sued?

5> Who will be your legal advisor?

Maxim: "You need a plan to build a house. To build a life, it is more important to have a plan or goal."
—*Zig Ziglar*

MYLEG ◄- -

MANAGEMENT**TEAM**

ABBREVIATION

MGMT

[Total Time Required: 45 Minutes]

STARTINGUP NOW DESCRIPTION

Introduce the management team by providing the
following information: Names, Titles, Direct Responsibilities,
Previous Experience, and Whom They Report To.

NATIONAL STANDARDS FOR ENTREPRENEURSHIP EDUCATION: CONTENT AREA(S) ADDRESSED

- J—Human Resource Management

---->

- Students will gain an understanding of the management team and its purpose.

  The management team's structure, style and integrity will define the culture of the business. It's necessary that the management team creates a productive environment for all involved to thrive. Proper management will help establish a productive business environment.

- **Model** ----> Review the model of Custom Bikes MGMT Team noting the various titles, areas of responsibilities, and reporting relationship of each "Team Member."

- **Activity** ----> Have students role-play the various roles and identify the potential challenges that may arise if a team member "plays" the wrong position. Then list how those challenges might impact the business.

- **SU Plan** ----> Students will complete the leadership tree identifying the various roles, responsibilities, experience levels, and reporting relationships for their businesses. (Students can add their own additional levels as needed.)

Research additional management structure resources, models of management, and management principles for the business. Research key principles from the Top 500 Best Managed Companies and identify common traits.

StartingUp Now Book, computer, Internet access, paper, pen/pencil, poster paper, and marker to recreate the leadership tree for their teams

STARTINGUP KEY 9

Description: *Introduce the management team by providing the following information: Name(s) and Title(s), Direct Responsibilities, Previous Experience, and Whom They Report To.*

Models

Custom Bikes MGMT Team

Julian Millard, Owner—Julian is responsible for all aspects of Custom Bikes, design, manufacturing, and client relations. Julian has been in the biking industry for over 20 years and has won numerous industry awards. Julian reports to Custom Bikes' investors.

Omar Reyes, Designer—Omar creates custom bike designs for customers desiring unique bicycles. Omar's designs have won awards for the past 10 years. Omar reports to the Owner.

Megan Smith, Dir. of Advertising—Megan is responsible for the design of all print and web-based advertising tools. Megan has worked at Custom Bikes for the last three years and reports to the Director of Sales.

Chelesta Falcone, Sales—Chelesta is responsible for managing independent sales reps throughout the United States and Canada. Chelesta has worked at Custom Bikes for the past six months and reports to the Owner.

> **StartUp Key 9:** Your company's management structure and style will define its culture. Your leadership team should create and foster a productive environment for growth and communication. Establishing accountability early is critical for productive business operations.

Use the following leadership structure (1–5) to help establish the person, his or her position, and whom he or she reports to. Substitute the appropriate position titles as you see fit.

1> Owner/CEO

2> Finance/Accounting

KEEP IT GOING LEARN STRATEGIES TO DEVELOP YOUR LEADERSHIP SKILLS AT WWW.STARTINGUPNOW.COM.

3> Sales/Marketing

4> Operations

5> Customer Relations

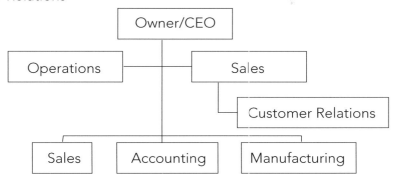

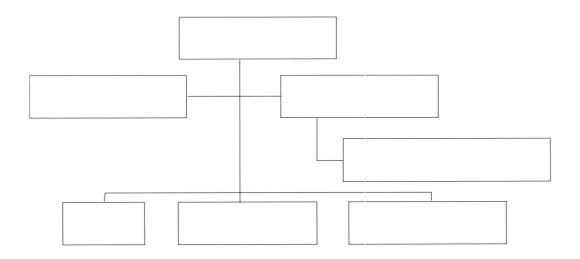

Maxim: "Leadership is the essence of any organized structure.
Leaders must lead, follow, or get out of the way."
—*Thomas Paine*

STARTINGUPPLAN 10

[Total Time Required: 45 Minutes]

STARTINGUP NOW DESCRIPTION

Your business goals should be attainable yet compel you to work hard to realize them. Goals provide specific focus that can be measured over a period of time. Achieving goals gives a sense of accomplishment and positive energy.

NATIONAL STANDARDS FOR ENTREPRENEURSHIP EDUCATION: CONTENT AREA(S) ADDRESSED

- O—Strategic Management
- N—Risk Management

- Students will grasp the concept that business success requires planning, execution, and assessment. This is especially important for a new business.

- Students will assess their plans and make adjustments at "halftime" in hopes of a victory. YOGA is analogous to a football team that establishes a scripted out game plan, play by play, for the first quarter.

- Students will script out their YOGAs to help evaluate the performance of their businesses over a specified period of time.

Performance Objectives ---->

- **Model** ----> Review the Lincoln Cafe's short- and long-term goals. Identify the distinctions between the time periods.

- **Activity** ----> Students will establish goals for their businesses in short, succinct bullet points.
  ----> Students will establish a deadline for the goals to be achieved.
  ----> Students must be able to explain why achieving the goals is important to the businesses.

- **SU Plan** ----> Students will list potential obstacles that may prevent them from achieving their goals.
  ----> Students will list out what they expect to learn from achieving the goals and how that learning might impact their planning abilities.

StartingUp Skill Center Application ---->

Research goal setting techniques via the SUSC. Identify specific goal-setting skills that can be incorporated for your business for either short- or long-term success. Share your goal-setting tips with those in your network or the broader SUSC global community.

Materials Needed ---->

StartingUp Now Book, computer, Internet access, poster-sized paper to record group/ team-based discussion notes

ABBREVIATION
YOGA

STARTINGUP KEY 10

Description: *Your business goals should be attainable yet compel you to work hard to realize them. Goals provide specific focus that can be measured over a period of time. Achieving goals gives a sense of accomplishment and positive energy.*

Models

The Lincoln Café Goals

Short-Term Goals (1–6 months):

> Secure monthly lease in strategic location to operate

> Hire one hosts, five waiters/waitresses, three cooks

> Identify 100 weekly repeat customers

> Break Even by 2nd Quarter

Long-Term Goals 6 months–1 year):

> Grow my weekly repeat customer base to 200 customers

> Sign a three-year lease with an option to purchase location

> Hire restaurant manager with at least five years of experience

> Generate $25,000 in net profits

StartUp Step 10: Use the following directions to guide the process for determining your goals for each of the time periods listed below.

1> Articulate your goals.

2> Identify the benchmarks to achieving your goals.
Describe your goals and be as specific as possible.

3> Establish a deadline for the goal to be completed.

4> Explain why achieving the goals will be important
to the business.

5> Recognize obstacles that may prevent you from
achieving each goal.

6> Upon successfully completing the goal, identify what you learned.

KEEP IT
GOING
READ ABOUT HOW OTHER COMPANIES DETERMINE THEIR
GOALS **AT WWW.STARTINGUPNOW.COM.**

Maxim: "Many are the plans in a man's heart, but
it is the LORD's purpose that prevails."
—*Proverbs 19:21, New International Version*

MY**YOGA**

STARTINGUP PLAN 11

ABBREVIATION

MIA

[Total Time Required: 45 Minutes]

STARTINGUP NOW DESCRIPTION

Investors need to know what's happening in your industry. Provide information on industry potential, competition, growth, and innovations. This is your opportunity to demonstrate your expertise and communicate the business opportunity.

NATIONAL STANDARDS FOR ENTREPRENEURSHIP EDUCATION: CONTENT AREA(S) ADDRESSED

- K—Information Analysis
- L—Marketing Management
- M—Operations Management
- O—Strategic Management

- Students will demonstrate expert knowledge of their particular industries. They ARE the resident experts and must present the business opportunities that exist based on their careful research.

- **Model** ----> Lead students in a discussion about how to identify the number of competing businesses there are in their industries.

- **Activity** ----> Students will identify the number of existing competing businesses in their industries along with key industry leaders.
  ----> Students will identify how much revenue their industries generate annually.
  ----> Students will identify their business' positions in their industries.

- **SU Plan** ----> Students will research then list government regulations for their industries.
  ----> Students will identify threats to their industries.
  ----> Students will identify foreseeable changes in the industries' immediate futures.

Students will research their particular industries and use the information gained from completing the Performance Objectives. Students can incorporate the knowledge gained into their business plans, share and rank knowledge pathways for other SUSC members, and refer others to their sources.

StartingUp Now Book, computer, Internet access to the SU Business Plan

INDUSTRY**ANALYSIS**

ABBREVIATION
MIA

Description: Investors need to know what's happening in your industry. Provide information on industry potential, competition, growth, and innovations.

Model

Red Line Race Works (Atlanta): Industry Trends for Slot Car Racing

Model slot car racing is a reemerging industry for model car racing hobbyists. It was first popularized in the '60s and gained visibility as commercial tracks sprung up in the U.S. and throughout Europe. The 1/32 scale is the most popular scale at this present time. There are approximately nine commercial tracks in the Atlanta area that range in size from 30–250 square feet. Scalextric, which is distributed by Hornby, controls about 70% of the U.S. market while other industry leaders, such as Carrera, Slot-It, and Fly, make up the balance. There is little government regulation as this is a very safe and non-technical industry. As we prepare to open three additional locations in the Charlotte, Orlando, and Birmingham areas, we will also introduce web-based racing simulations.

StartUp Step 11: Use the following questions to serve as a guide to identify the trends in your industry.

1> How many businesses are in your industry?

2> How much revenue does your industry generate annually?

3> Who are the industry leaders?

4> What is your position in the industry?

5> What are the existing government regulations for your industry?

6> Are there any threats to the industry?

7> Are there any foreseeable changes in your industry's immediate future?

KEEP IT GOING COLLECT INDUSTRY-SPECIFIC INTELLIGENCE AND SHARE YOUR EXPERIENCE **AT WWW.STARTINGUPNOW.COM.**

Maxim: Tell your story. What do you know about this industry that will give you a competitive edge? By telling your story and your niche, you can also provide an effective, passionate analysis of your industry that's both compelling and informative.

MY**IA**

_____
_____
_____
_____
_____
_____
_____
_____
_____
_____
_____
_____
_____
_____
_____
_____
_____
_____
_____
_____
_____
_____
_____
_____
_____

MAR**KETING**

[Total Time Required: 60 Minutes]

STARTINGUP NOW DESCRIPTION

MARKETING is the activities and methods that business owners use to sell their products or services to their customers. In order to have a solid business plan, a business owner MUST conduct market research.

NATIONAL STANDARDS FOR ENTREPRENEURSHIP EDUCATION: CONTENT AREA(S) ADDRESSED

• L—Marketing Management

---->

- Students will gain an understanding of the importance of marketing.

  Marketing is the research element that students must complete to validate the existence of the business. A poor marketing plan often results in a poor business operation—literally. Students must "justify" the sustainability of the business based upon current market conditions. If the marketing data does not provide an opportunity for a successful business operation—students must assess these factors prior to starting the business.

Performance Objectives ---->

- **Model** ----> Review West Side Geeks data gained from their market research specifically focusing on the "6 Ps" of Marketing.
  ----> Discuss what their marketing data revealed about their potential customer base and how the information gained can be useful in developing their business strategy.

- **Activity** ----> Using the 6 Ps and the marketing chart, complete market research for your particular business with 3 different companies that sell a product/service similar to yours.

- **SU Plan** ----> Students should use the 6 Ps as a guide to secure data needed to create their own marketing plans for their businesses.
  ----> Use the StartingUp Now template to write out your marketing plan or enter the information on the StartingUp Now Online Business Plan.

StartingUp Skill Center Application ---->

Review additional marketing research methodologies that are often used by businesses in your industry or others that can help you gain the data/intelligence needed to help position your business for success. Feel free to share tips, techniques, and sources to others on the SUSC network.

Materials Needed ---->

No materials are needed at this time.

STARTINGUP KEY 12

Description: *Marketing is the activities and methods that business owners use to sell their products or services to their customers. In order to have a solid business plan, the business owner must conduct market research.*

Model
West Side Geeks, Inc.

West Side Geeks, Inc., is conducting market research to determine if their idea of refurbishing and reselling pre-owned computers will lead to a profitable business. In order to determine their likelihood of success, they must research their potential market. What they learn from their market research will help create effective marketing strategies, techniques, and tools needed to communicate the value of their product or service to potential customers.

The 6 Ps of Marketing: People, Product, Price, Place, Promotion, and Presentation will help West Side Geeks, Inc., learn more about their market. Here's a brief description of the 6 Ps of Marketing.

1> **People**—Undervaluing people in your business activities will likely lead to the failure of the business. What do they need your product or service to do? How are they valued in the process?

2> **Product**—Clearly identify what you are selling. Is it a product/service? How will the customer benefit from the product/service?

3> **Price**—How much are customers willing to pay? How much are they currently paying for the same or a similar product?

4> **Place**—Where are customers currently purchasing the same or similar service?

5> **Promotion**—How is the product/service currently being promoted?

6> **Presentation**—How and where is the product/service being presented?

By researching the 6 Ps of Marketing, West Side Geeks, Inc., learned the following about their potential market:

People	> Parents value their children's education.
	> They want to purchase an affordable computer for their children to do their homework and use online educational tools.
	> Most parents are lower to middle income and work full time.
Product	> Customers want a reliable desktop computer that includes keyboard, mouse, display, CPU.
	> A major brand is helpful but not necessary.
	> Some level of product support and warranty is desired— especially for refurbished computers.
	> Installation of and networking the computer would be helpful.
Price	> Customers are willing to pay $350–$600 for a desktop computer.
	> Some customers purchase on credit or layaway.
Place	> Currently most customers purchase only from big box retailers.
Promotion	> Big box retailers run weekly ads in local newspapers and advertise using social media.
	> Flyers, business cards, and other advertising tools
Presentation	> Packaging used is not environmentally responsible.
	> Some computer components are manufactured with products that are harmful to the environment.

Let's perform market research for your own business. Using the chart on the following page as a guide, research 2–3 companies that offer the same/similar products and services just as West Side Geeks, Inc., did.

MARKETING

	COMPANY 1	COMPANY 2	COMPANY 3
People:			
Product:			
Price:			
Place:			
Promotion:			
Presentation:			

KEEP IT GOING

JOIN THE COMMUNITY OF NEW ENTREPRENEURS AT WWW.STARTINGUPNOW.COM.

People:

Product:

Price:

Place:

Promotion:

Presentation:

Maxim: "Strategy without tactics is the slowest route to victory. Tactics without strategy is the noise before defeat."
—*Sun Tzu*

TARGET**CUSTOMER PROFILE**

ABBREVIATION

TCP

[Total Time Required: 45–90 Minutes]

STARTINGUP NOW DESCRIPTION

An expert understanding of your customers and prospects is critical to developing your sales strategy and future development of new products and services.

NATIONAL STANDARDS FOR ENTREPRENEURSHIP EDUCATION: CONTENT AREA(S) ADDRESSED

- D—Communications/Interpersonal Skills
- L—Marketing Management

---->

Learning Objectives ---->

- Students will learn how to assess their customers' needs and desires. Gaining this information will help them to cater their business products/services to meet their customers' needs.

Performance Objectives ---->

- **Models** ----> Students will review the Meraz Miniature Golf (MMG) Customer Profile, ascertaining the various facts presented about MMG customers.
  - ----> Ask open ended questions such as:
  - ----> "How does the information presented by MMG helps them run their business?"
  - ----> "Who is MMG's competition? How close are they?"

- **Activity** ----> Students must complete all the StartUp Steps to help them create a "profile" of their own target customers.

- **SU Plan** ----> Upon completing the StartUp Steps, students should list out their Target Customers Profiles in their StartingUp Now business plan templates or on their business plans online.
  - ----> Students should also demo how their businesses will meet their customers' needs.

StartingUp Skill Center Application ---->

Research Target Customer Profile and read customer profiles and studies. Additional resources and methodologies performed by other SUSC members will likely benefit your business directly. Feel free to share, post, and assess other related resources with the SUSC community.

Materials Needed ---->

StartingUp Now Book, pencil/pen, computer, Internet access, access to potential customers to perform the TCP

ABBREVIATION
TCP

STARTINGUP KEY 13

Description: *An expert understanding of your customers and prospects is critical to developing your sales strategy and future development of new products and services.*

Model

Meraz Miniature Golf (MMG) Customer Profile

MMG is a seasonal, family-owned-and-operated miniature golf complex located in a major metropolitan city with approximately 150,000 working families within a five-mile radius. Each year MMG attracts customers that are typically multi-ethnic families with an annual income of $40,000–$75,000 and have children between the ages of 5–12 years old. The average family of four will spend $25.00 on golfing and an additional $20.00 on food and beverages for 36 holes of golfing. MMG is often viewed as an affordable alternative that is in closer proximity than the major amusement park, which is about 40 miles away. MMG customers value a clean, safe, family-friendly environment that's affordable for working families. MMG also provides birthday parties, private and corporate events, and weekly contests, along with family membership passes throughout the summer.

StartUp Step 13: Let the following questions serve as a guide to create a profile of your customers.

1> What are the demographics of your target market: income level, age range, education level, disposable income, gender, race/ethnicity, location, etc.?

2> What are the psychographics of the target market: values, social class, lifestyle, and personality characteristics?

3> How large is your target market? Is this a niche/specialty market?

4> On what do your potential customers spend money?

5> From where do they currently purchase the product or service that you provide?

KEEP IT GOING

FOR ADDITIONAL RESOURCES AND IDEAS ON CREATING YOUR TARGET CUSTOMER PROFILE, LOG ON TO **WWW.STARTINGUPNOW.COM.**

Maxim: "With businesses, you go to the same places because you like the service, you like the people, and they take care of you. They greet you with a smile. That's how people want to be treated, with respect. That's what I tell my employees...customer service is very important."
—*Erving "Magic" Johnson*

MYTCP ◄

FEATURES& BENEFITS

ABBREVIATION

FAB

[Total Time Required: 30–45 Minutes]

STARTINGUP NOW DESCRIPTION

Highlighting the features and benefits of your product
or service is a necessity. It's important to identify multiple **FEATURES**
and show how the features will directly **BENEFIT** the customer.

NATIONAL STANDARDS FOR ENTREPRENEURSHIP EDUCATION: CONTENT AREA(S) ADDRESSED

- D—Communications/Interpersonal Skills
- L—Marketing Management

- Students will develop an understanding of FAB and gain experience presenting and relating it to their businesses.

  This is a fun exercise that can be performed with almost any common classroom/household item (i.e., a pen, a piece of paper, a computer). This can be repeated multiple times throughout the classroom to teach students how to "present" the feature and "turn" the feature into a direct benefit for the customer. Knowing how to articulate the FAB will lead to better sales presentations.

- **Model** ----> Read and review the Model of Disposable Pen with the students.
  - ----> On poster paper draw two columns,
  - ----> Label the left column "Features."
  - ----> Label the right column "Benefits." This should be similar to the diagram in StartUp Key 14.

- **Activity** ----> Use a disposable pen that you have to review how the Features of the pen directly Benefit the pen's owner.
  - ----> Have the students use other common items from your classroom and repeat the FAB exercise.

- **SU Plan** ----> Now, have the students complete the FAB exercise for their own products/services.
  - ----> Students should write out the FABs of their products/services in their business plan templates in their books or on their StartingUp Online Business Plans.

Read through the various Features and Benefits of SUSC members and products from the Marketing tab. Identifying how a business distinguishes the direct benefit of their products/services to be helpful. Several SUSC members in the community have similar businesses but may have different features for their markets. Research their models, best practices, and other resources and share with the SUSC network.

StartingUp Now Book, pen/pencil, poster paper for demo of disposable pen model, copy paper for students to do their own FAB exercise

Description: *Highlighting the features and benefits of your product or service is a necessity. It's important to identify multiple FEATURES and show how the features will directly BENEFIT the customer.*

Model

Disposable Pen:

FEATURES ····>	BENEFITS
Inexpensive ····>	Affordable to most consumers
Clip ····>	Attaches to pocket or folder
Disposable ····>	Inexpensive to own
Multiple colors of ink ····>	Various colors for different tasks
Small/Compact ····>	Easy to carry
Comes with a cap ····>	Reduces ink spillage
Name Brand ····>	Trustworthy brand/reliability
Sold at Retail Stores ····>	Available

StartUp Key 14: Identify the features and benefits of your product or service in the columns below:

FEATURES ····>	BENEFITS
····>	
····>	
····>	
····>	
····>	
····>	
····>	
····>	

KEEP IT GOING GAIN PRODUCT PROMOTION TECHNIQUES AND BEST PRACTICES AT WWW.STARTINGUPNOW.COM.

STARTINGUP KEY 14

Maxim: "Always be truth-telling. A half-truth is a whole lie."
—Yiddish Proverb

MYFAB ◄

SALES**STRATEGY**

ABBREVIATION

SELL

[Total Time Required: 30–45 Minutes]

STARTINGUP NOW DESCRIPTION

Developing your sales strategy is an essential task. As an entrepreneur, this is your opportunity to define your business's approach to prospect identification, account generation, and achieving sales targets.

NATIONAL STANDARDS FOR ENTREPRENEURSHIP EDUCATION: CONTENT AREA(S) ADDRESSED

- D—Communications/Interpersonal Skills
- L—Marketing Management
- M—Operations Management

---->

- Students will learn how to develop a sales presentation for their products or services. Students must know the Features & Benefits of their products to create a memorable sales pitch. Students should provide demos, samples, or testimonials of their products/services to make their sales pitches real!

Performance Objectives ---->

- **Model** ----> Students should read and review the CleanStic Toothpick sales pitch model.
  - ----> As the instructor, you can either read it aloud as if you/ they were really selling the CleanStic.
  - ----> Or select a student with strong verbal/communication skills to read it as a "sales pitch."
  - ----> Ensure the SELL tips are used in the presentation.

- **Activity** ----> Students can practice their SELLs with other items common to your classroom.

- **SU Plan** ----> Having seen this practiced 2–3 times, students must then create their own SELLs for their products or services.
  - ----> Students must write out their sales pitches in their StartingUp Now books or on the StartingUp Now online business plans.
  - ----> The SELL should be less than 1 minute and incorporate Features & Benefits.

StartingUp Skill Center Application ---->

There are multiple sales tips and techniques used by entrepreneurs. Oftentimes sales techniques vary depending on the customer. Wal-Mart allows only 15 minutes for an entrepreneur to sell a product. Research a few sales tips that can help overall presentation of your product/service. Share your insights, experiences, and knowledge gained with others in SUSC community.

Materials Needed ---->

No materials are needed at this time.

Description: *Developing your sales strategy is an essential task. As an entrepreneur, this is your opportunity to define your company's approach to prospect identification, account generation, and achieving sales targets.*

Model

CleanStic Toothpicks, Inc.

Tagline: Only clean the teeth you want to keep!

Sales Pitch: **CleanStic Toothpicks** provide oral hygiene cleanliness, breath enhancers, along with being environmentally safe. At the conclusion of each meal, simply remove the **CleanStic** from the biodegradable wrapping and swiftly clean the surfaces and crevices between your teeth. By removing excess particles of food, immediately patrons reduce the possible plaque buildup along with minimizing bad breath from food particles left in the mouth. Which flavor of **CleanStic** would you like to try?

StartUp Step 15:

> **S**how the feature and demonstrate how the feature works.

> **E**xplain how the customer will benefit from the advantage gained from the feature.

> **L**ead into the features and benefits. Demonstrate how it will benefit their direct needs.

> **L**et the customers talk among themselves about how the product will benefit them; if done correctly, they will talk themselves into a sell.

Maxim: "For every sale you miss because you're too enthusiastic, you'll miss a hundred because you are not enthusiastic enough. Every sale has five basic obstacles: no need, no money, no hurry, no desire, no trust."
—*Zig Ziglar*

KEEP IT GOING — LEARN ADDITIONAL SALES TIPS AND STRATEGIES ONLINE AT WWW.STARTINGUPNOW.COM.

STARTINGUP KEY 15

MY**COMPETITION**

ABBREVIATION
COMP

[Total Time Required: 45–90 Minutes]

STARTINGUP NOW DESCRIPTION

Knowing your competition provides valuable information—especially in the startup phase. Identifying each competitor's strengths and weaknesses allows you to demonstrate why customers will select your product over your competitors. Knowing your competition will allow for better knowledge of your industry and target customer.

NATIONAL STANDARDS FOR ENTREPRENEURSHIP EDUCATION: CONTENT AREA(S) ADDRESSED

- F—Economics: Understands the economic principles and concepts fundamental to entrepreneurship/small business ownership.

---->

- Students will learn that it is important to know their competition as a business owners—but not become distracted by their competition. Focusing on their strengths, improving their weaknesses, while being cognizant of the competition is vital.

- **Model** ----> Students should read and review the Model comparing and contrasting purchasing a toaster. They should note the differences in purchasing the toaster from each location.

- **Activity** ----> Select three students. Assign each student to represent one of the three locations. Have each student create a SELL based on the parameters for each location. Have the rest of the class vote on which competitor provided the best sales pitch.
  ----> Students should complete the exercises in StartUp Key 16. This will enable them to identify their competition and identify their own competitive advantages.

- **SU Plan** ----> Students should write out their specific competitive advantages and list those in the business plan templates in their books or on their online plans. Instruct students to use their competitive advantages in order for their businesses to compete in the marketplace.

Look up My Competition on the SUSC to learn strategies needed to compete in the industry's market place. Investigate how leading companies deal with their competition (McDonald's vs. Wendy's). What makes some companies thrive while others have failed? Share your findings with those in the network and industry, and then rate available content.

No materials are needed at this time.

STARTINGUP KEY 16

Description: *Knowing your competition provides valuable information. You must know who they are and where they are located. Identifying each competitor's strengths and weaknesses allows you to demonstrate why customers will select your product over your competitors. Knowing your competition will allow for better knowledge of your industry and target customer.*

Model

Below is a chart highlighting the competitive differences between three stores that retail similar products. There are pros and cons to purchasing the product from one or the other.

Product: Toaster	Local Store	National Chain	Specialty Store
Quality	Average	Good	Excellent
Reputation	Good	Average	Excellent
Customer Service	Good	Below Average	Excellent
Selection	1–3	1–10	1–5
Price Point	$15.00–$30.00	$10.00–$40.00	$40.00–$200.00
Product Knowledge	Average	Below Average	Excellent

StartUp Key 16: In order to best compete with your competition, use the following steps to analyze your competition and let's prepare your strategy to compete:

1> Who currently sells the same or similar product or service as you?

2> What is the size of the target market?

3> What factors are most important to the customers when making a decision (price, quality, selection, warranty, etc.)?

Maxim: "Make your product easier to buy than your competition, or you will find your customers buying from them, not you."
—*Mark Cuban*

KEEP IT GOING NEED ADDITIONAL STRATEGIES TO DEAL WITH YOUR COMPETITION? VISIT **WWW.STARTINGUPNOW.COM** TO LEARN MORE.

S.W.O.T.S.

ABBREVIATION

S.W.O.T.S.

[Total Time Required: 30–45 Minutes]

STARTINGUP NOW DESCRIPTION

Identifying and acting on your advantages is a useful strategy not only in starting your business, but also in order to remain competitive in the marketplace. We often spend far too much time focusing on our weaknesses versus recognizing and building on our strengths.

NATIONAL STANDARDS FOR ENTREPRENEURSHIP EDUCATION: CONTENT AREA(S) ADDRESSED

- B—Entrepreneurial Traits/Behaviors: Understand the personal traits/behaviors associated with successful entrepreneurial performances.

---->

Learning Objective ---->

- Students will learn that their strengths are one of their key assets. While many spend time trying to improve their weaknesses, they run the risk of neglecting their strengths. A S.W.O.T.S. analysis will help identify their market position and grow their strengths, while being fully aware of areas that need improvement.

Performance Objectives ---->

- **Models** ----> Read and review Prime Ribs and their S.W.O.T.S. analysis. Students should note what Prime Ribs learned about their business model from their own S.W.O.T.S. analysis.
  ----> Ask open ended questions that will lead to discussions on how a S.W.O.T.S. analysis benefits an entrepreneur.

- **Activity** ----> Students should memorize the definition for S.W.O.T.S. and perform a S.W.O.T.S. analysis for their own businesses—even though it may not be operational yet.
  ----> Additionally, students may want to present their own S.W.O.T.S. analyses to the group on poster paper.
  ----> S.W.O.T.S. analyses can be used multiple times throughout the life of the business.

- **SU Plan** ----> Students will write out their S.W.O.T.S. analyses for their companies on their templates or on their SU Online Business Plans.

StartingUp Skill Center Application ---->

- Look up S.W.O.T.S. and identify how companies have listed their own S.W.O.T.S. Seek out characteristics that may be similar to yours and/or how a business uses a particular S.W.O.T.S. that may be similar or different to yours. Identify resources such as books, videos, and links to web-based resources that other SUSC members can review. Post content that will serve the larger SUSC community.

- Students will save their research under their profiles for future access.

Materials Needed ---->

StartingUp Now Book, pen/pencil, poster paper, computer, Internet access

STARTINGUP KEY 17

➤ S.W.O.T.S.

ABBREVIATION
S.W.O.T.S.

Description: *Identifying and acting on your advantages is a useful strategy not only in starting your business but also in order to remain competitive in the marketplace. We often spend far too much time focusing on our weaknesses versus recognizing and building on our strengths.*

Models

Prime Ribs management is accessing their marketplace positions through a S.W.O.T.S. analysis. Below is their internal S.W.O.T.S. review:

S.W.O.T.S.	Prime Ribs S.W.O.T.S. Analysis
Strengths: Identify all of your strengths that positively impact your business.	> Profitable & Well-Organized > Family-Friendly Reputation > National Awards > Secret Sauce/Recipe
Weaknesses: Identify your areas of weakness that need to be improved.	> Limited Access to Capital > Small Location > Employee Turnover
Opportunities: Which opportunities exist that can improve your business?	> Small Business Loan > Expansion to 2nd Location > Retail Sauce in Grocery Stores
Threats: Identify internal/external threats that could negatively impact your business.	> Lack of Access to Capital > New construction project impacting traffic flow
Strategies: List out your strategies to overcome your weaknesses and minimize your threats.	> Sell 30% of business to secure investment capital > Increase hourly wage to reduce turnover

KEEP IT GOING — LEARN MORE ABOUT "STRENGTH COACHING AND TECHNIQUES" AT WWW.STARTINGUPNOW.COM.

S.W.O.T.S.	My Business
Strengths: Identify all of your strengths that positively impact your business.	> > > >
Weaknesses: Identify your areas of weakness that need to be improved.	> > >
Opportunities: Which opportunities exist that can improve your business?	> > >
Threats: Identify internal/external threats that could negatively impact your business.	> >
Strategies: List out your strategies to overcome your weaknesses and minimize your threats.	> >

Maxim: "It doesn't matter who you are or where you come from.
The ability to triumph begins with you. Always."
—*Oprah Winfrey*

MY**S.W.O.T.S.** ◄- -

_____
_____
_____
_____
_____
_____
_____
_____

MY**ADVERTISING**

[Total Time Required: 30–90 Minutes]

↓

STARTINGUP NOW DESCRIPTION

Advertising is truthfully communicating a message to persuade customers to purchase your product or service.

↓

NATIONAL STANDARDS FOR ENTREPRENEURSHIP EDUCATION: CONTENT AREA(S) ADDRESSED

- C—Business Foundations
- L—Marketing Management

---->

- Students will learn to create an advertisement theme for their products/services. Their TCPs will help determine the type of AD they will use to engage potential customers. Creating a 30-Second AD should be fun and exciting for the business owner! It allows the businesses to make an announcement to the marketplace about who they are.

Performance Objectives ---->

- **Model** ----> Read and review the TAZE ad with the students. Review with students the importance of honesty in communicating what a product can/cannot do.
  - ----> Have students identify and write out the similarities of the TAZE ad to other ads they may see on television, Facebook, etc.
  - ----> Assign students to list out how TAZE claims it will benefit the customer.

- **Activity** ----> Students will write out a script for a 30-Second Ad using the steps in StartUp Key 18.
  - ----> Upon completing their ads, students will perform/ act out their ads to the class.
  - ----> If possible, record the ad as part of your ad campaign.

- **SU Plan** ----> Use the ad as part of your ad campaign for your business plan.

StartingUp Skill Center Application ---->

Research the methods in which businesses, large and small, advertise their products/services. Determine if these methods will work for your business. Seek out techniques and sources that may help you. If you discover helpful information, post it for the SUSC community to review.

Materials Needed ---->

StartingUp Book, pen/pencil, computer, Internet access, video camera or mobile device with a video recorder, SUSC Membership

ABBREVIATION
AD

STARTINGUP KEY 18

Description: *Advertising is truthfully communicating a message to persuade customers to purchase your product or service.*

Model
Product: TAZE!
Slogan: Power Drinks for Triathletes
Tagline: Get Your TAZE ON!

Script: Train harder, run faster, swim longer, bike harder—outlast your competition with TAZE Power Drinks.

> **StartUp Step 18:** Advertising often takes the form of television and radio commercials, Facebook and YouTube banner ads, slogans, brochures, and business cards. Use the following questions to help you create a memorable, truthful ad about your product or service.

Create a 30-Second Ad:

    1> Identify your product/service that you are selling.

    2> Create a slogan that ties in with your product/service.

    3> Create a memorable tagline that they won't forget.

    4> Write out the script. Keep it short; you only have 30 seconds.

    5> Perform the ad. If needed, use friends and props.

    6> Record the ad with a video or webcam.

    7> Edit the ad with simple software and post it on YouTube.

Hint: Use your FAB & SELL sections to complete your commercial.

> **Maxim:** "Do not deceive one another."
> *—Leviticus 19:11, New International Version*

KEEP IT GOING   CHECK OUT OTHER ADVERTISING TOOLS AND TECHNIQUES AT WWW.STARTINGUPNOW.COM.

STARTUP**COSTS**

[Total Time Required: 45–90 Minutes]

STARTING**UP** NOW DESCRIPTION

Start-up cost is the amount of money needed to purchase
the items necessary to start your business.

NATIONAL STANDARDS FOR ENTREPRENEURSHIP EDUCATION: CONTENT AREA(S) ADDRESSED

- C—Business Foundations
- F—Economics
- G—Financial Literacy
- I—Financial Management
- M—Operations Management

---->

- Students will research and list the items needed to start their businesses. The simplicity or complexity of the businesses will help determine what they need to get started. Upon completing this lesson, students will learn how to:
  - Research start-up items needed for their businesses
  - Assign a monetary value for the items
  - Create an inventory list
  - Track the quantity of items needed
  - Learn about wholesale discounts

Performance Objectives ---->

- **Model** ----> Read and review Old Time Lemonade's start-up costs. Direct students to Michelle's specific goal to make $500.00 in sales.

- **Activity** ----> With their books closed, inform students you are considering starting a lemonade stand/business in their classroom as a project.
  - ----> Have students begin to identify the items needed for the business. Identify quantities and prices.
  - ----> Have students open their books to see if their lists are similar to that of Old Time Lemonade's.
  - ----> Students should complete all the tasks in StartUp Step 19 for their own business efforts by using the chart.
  - ----> Students will note that their Wholesale Discount Percentage will vary from 30–60% off typical retail prices.

- **SU Plan** ----> Using the chart, students will list all the items needed to launch their businesses as part of their start-up costs. It's necessary for students to perform their best research and narrow down the amount of money needed to get started. Their total start-up costs are key factors in their Financial Plans.

StartingUp Skill Center Application ---->

Determining start-up cost is your best estimate based on the research you've conducted. Your business type, industry regulations, and the willingness of business owners to share prices from their suppliers (oftentimes this is quite sensitive) will all help determine how accessible this information will be to you. Determining your start-up costs is often viewed as more of an art than a science. Log in to the SUSC discover models, charts, and related articles to help with your start-up costs.

Materials Needed ---->

No materials are needed at this time.

STARTUP**COSTS**

Description: *Start-up cost is the amount of money needed to purchase the items necessary to start your business.*

Models

Michelle of Old Time Lemonade is setting up "just outside the fence" of a professional football team's training camp facility in the Midwest. Many fans visit the facility to watch the team practice. Michelle wants to make $500.00 in one day to purchase a new computer for the upcoming school year. Below, she's listed the items needed to start the lemonade stand. She's selling her lemonade for $3.00 per cup—no free refills.

Old Time Lemonade Start-up Costs:

Item	Unit Cost	Quantity	Total
Lemons	.20 each	20	$4.00
Bottled Water	$2.00	20	$40.00
Pitcher	$3.00	2	$6.00
Mixing Spoon	$1.00	2	$2.00
Signage for Posters	$1.00	5	$5.00
Lemonade Mix	$5.00	5	$25.00
Cups (12 oz.)	$3.00	8 (24 in pkg.)	$24.00
Ice (20 lb. bag)	$3.00	2	$6.00
Table & 2 Chairs	$20.00	1	$20.00
Hourly Pay Rate	$5.00	8	$40.00
Total			$172.00

StartUp Step 19: The questions and chart to the right will guide you through the beginning stages of determining your Start-up Costs.

1> Create a list of all the items you need to get your business started for one month. This will be the beginning of your inventory list.

KEEP IT GOING   JOIN THE COMMUNITY OF NEW ENTREPRENEURS AT WWW.STARTINGUPNOW.COM.

2> Next, write down the quantity of the items needed for each of the items.

3> List out the approximate costs next to each of the items.

4> Typically, when you are a *licensed* business owner reselling a product or service, you can receive a *wholesale* discount that ranges from 30–60% off retail price. These discounts typically apply when you purchase in *bulk* quantities. List out the *vendor's* name and the discount percentage they are offering you.

Item	Unit Cost	Quantity	Vendor	Discount %	Sub-Total

MYSUC ◄--

OPERATIONAL**EXPENSES**

ABBREVIATION
OPEX

[Total Time Required: 60 Minutes]

STARTINGUP NOW DESCRIPTION

Operational expenses are the budgeted costs that are incurred in order for the business to remain functional. These expenses typically occur monthly regardless how many products or services the business sells. OPEX is often referred to as Fixed Costs or Overhead Expenses because they occur each month.

NATIONAL STANDARDS FOR ENTREPRENEURSHIP EDUCATION: CONTENT AREA(S) ADDRESSED

- C—Business Foundations
- F—Economics
- G—Financial Literacy
- I—Financial Management
- M—Operations Management

---->

- Students will learn the USAIIRM acronym to help determine their monthly OPEXs. Upon learning their OPEX students will be able to intelligently establish the prices of their products/services.

- Students will create a monthly budget and project both short- and long-term expenses.

Performance Objectives ---->

- **Model** ----> Read and review High End Fashions OPEX. Review each of the USAIIRM categories, ensuring students know the definition, order, and direct impact for the OPEX.

- **Activity** ----> Quiz students on the definition/order.
  ----> Assign various dollar amounts to each category and have students calculate the monthly OPEX.

  ----> **SU Step 20:** Students must complete all the steps in this lesson to determine their OPEXs. This will be a time-consuming process that will require a few hours of research depending on the level and type of business. However, the quality of their research and fact-finding will lead toward more successful business plans.

- **SU Plan** ----> Once students complete their OPEX research, they should enter their USAIIRM expenses on the chart in the SU book template or online business plan.

StartingUp Skill Center Application ---->

Managing OPEX is an art that all business owners seek to master. Research strategies and standard operating procedures that have worked for other business owners. Watch video clips of SUSC members that are willing to share tips, tricks, and techniques they use to manage operational expenses.

Materials Needed ---->

StartingUp Book, pen/pencil, computer, Internet access, SUSC Membership

OPERATIONALEXPENSES

ABBREVIATION
OPEX

Description: *Operational expenses are the budgeted costs that are incurred in order for the business to remain functional. These expenses typically occur each month regardless of how many products or services the business sells. OPEX is often referred to as Fixed Costs because they occur each month. For example, whether a clothing store sells 50 or 500 shirts, the store must pay rent each month. Knowing and planning for your monthly operational expenses is vital for operations. OPEX are also called Overhead.*

Model

High End Fashions, LLC., is a used clothing store that sells only the latest women's fashions. It is extremely important for High End to know its OPEX to effectively budget and plan for future months. See the example below.

USAIIRM	Description	High End USAIIRM
for June		
U-tilities	Electric, Gas, Phone, Cell, Internet	$300.00
S-alaries	Employee Payroll & Payroll Taxes	$2,000.00
A-dvertising	Ads, Coupons, Web Banner Ads, etc.	$500.00
I-nsurance	General Insurance for the business	$50.00
I-nterest	Business Loan Payments	$100.00
R-ent	Rent or Mortgage Payment	$500.00
M-iscellaneous	Uncategorized Expenses	$50.00
Total		$3,500.00

The owners of High End Fashions know that each month their operational expenses will be at least $3500. Knowing their operational expenses helps to create a strategy in order for the business to be profitable.

StartUp Step 20: Use USAIIRM to budget your monthly operational expenses with the chart on the right. Use the following questions to get started:

1> What will I spend on utilities each month?

KEEP IT GOING

JOIN THE COMMUNITY OF NEW ENTREPRENEURS AT WWW.STARTINGUPNOW.COM.

2> How much will I budget for salaries each month?

3> Do I plan to advertise this month? If so, how much will I budget?

4> How much will the business spend per month on insurance expenses?

5> If the business has a loan, how much needs to be paid back per month?

6> How much is your rent each month?

7> Do you want to budget a certain amount for uncategorized expenses? If so, how much?

Maxim: "Take care of the pennies and the dollars will take care of themselves."
—*William Lowndes, U.S. Congressman*

U-tilities	Budgeted Amount
S-alaries	
A-dvertising	
I-nsurance	
I-nterest	
R-ent	
M-iscellaneous	
Total	

MYOPEX ◄ -

COST OF GOODS

ABBREVIATION
COG

[Total Time Required: 60–120 Minutes]

STARTINGUP NOW DESCRIPTION

Knowing your **COST OF GOODS** (COG) is essential for setting the prices of your products or services. COG is the cost the business pays to make the products/services available. COG typically includes the cost of things such as material and labor.

NATIONAL STANDARDS FOR ENTREPRENEURSHIP EDUCATION: CONTENT AREA(S) ADDRESSED

- C—Business Foundations
- F—Economics
- I—Financial Management

---->

- Students will learn how to effectively price their products/services factoring in their wholesale discounted costs.

- Students will learn how to price out items consumed in the performance of a job, which is particularly important in a service based business.

- Students will learn that a business owner "marks up" the cost of the product in order to make a profit.

- **Model** ----> Read and review Jamal's Donuts with the students.
  ----> Students will discuss the differences between product based and service-based businesses:
    ----> Product-Based Businesses—sell a product that you can usually touch (Jamal's Donuts).
    ----> Service-Based Business—sells a service that you provide (DSX Deck Washing).

- **Activity** ----> For a product based business, students will use a Product-Based Formula for each product they plan to sell.
  ----> Product-Based Pricing Formula=Retail Price(a)–COGs(b)=Gross Profit (c)
  ----> Service-Based Pricing Formula=Retail Price(a)–COS(b)=Gross Profit (c)

- **SU Plan** ----> Students must first determine if they are product based, service based, or a combination. Upon making that determination they must then cost out each of their COGs or COSs for each product they sell.
  ----> Direct the students to use the chart in Step 21 on their business plan templates or on the online business plan templates.

N/A

No materials are needed at this time.

STARTINGUP KEY 21

Description: *Knowing your Cost of Goods (COG) is essential for setting the prices of your products or services. COG is the cost the business pays to make the products/services available. COG typically includes the cost of things such as material and labor.*

Models

Jamal's Donuts

Jamal sells donuts at school. Jamal sells his donuts for $1.00 each (a). Jamal purchases donuts wholesale on average for about $0.30 per donut (b). Therefore, Jamal's COG is $0.30 per unit, and he makes $0.70 in *gross profit* (c).

Retail Price (a) - COGs (b) = Gross Profit (c)

Jamal's COGs		
Donut Retail Price	$1.00	a
Cost of Goods Sold	$0.30	b
Gross Profit per donut	$0.70	c

DSX Wooden Deck Washing Service

David and Shawn own and operate a deck washing service. DSX sells a service (deck washing) but must include the cost of supplies (products) needed to clean the decks. They charge $100.00 per deck (a). The hourly rate they pay themselves is $10.00 per hour (b), and it takes two hours to perform the service (c) for a total labor cost of $20.00 per person (d). The men must also factor in the cost of supplies (e) needed to perform the job, and they *mark up* their supply cost by 15% (f). They combine their supply cost and markup percentage (g) to get their total supply cost of $57.50. By subtracting their COS (h) from their retail price (a), their gross profit is $22.50 (i).

KEEP IT GOING — LEARN MORE ABOUT OPERATIONAL EXPENSES AT WWW.STARTINGUPNOW.COM.

DSX Cost of Services (COS)		
Deck Washing Retail Price	$100.00	a
Labor Cost Per Hour	$10.00	b
How Many Hours To Perform Service	2	c
Total Labor Cost	$20.00	d
Cost of Supplies	$10.00	e
Supplies Markup 15%	$5.00	f
Supplies + Markup	$15.50	g
Cost of Services Sold	$35.50	h
Gross Profit	$65.50	i

They combine their supply cost and markup percentage (e+f) to get their total supply and labor cost of $35.00 (h). Now, by subtracting their Total Supply & Labor Cost (a-i), they get their gross profit of $65.00 (i).

MYCOG ◄--

INCOMESTATEMENT

ABBREVIATION
INST

[Total Time Required: 45–90 Minutes]

STARTINGUP NOW DESCRIPTION

The **INCOME STATEMENT** reports on the amount of revenue
a company has earned over a specific period of time. The INST allows
the business owner to review detailed information on where the business
is making or losing money. The INST can be thought of as a "score sheet"
providing real-time data on how the business is doing. The INST is also
referred to as the Profit & Loss Statement (P & L).

NATIONAL STANDARDS FOR ENTREPRENEURSHIP EDUCATION: CONTENT AREA(S) ADDRESSED

- C—Business Foundations
- F—Economics
- I—Financial Management

---->

- Students will learn the key role the INST plays in their business plans and the ongoing role it plays in their business operations.
- Students will learn how to complete each of the steps in order to complete INSTs for their own businesses.

- **Model** ----> Students will review the Green Acres Landscaping INST. Students will learn the categories, definitions, and order of the INST.

  ----> Using the operational steps in StartUp Step 22 as a guide, have students answer each of the questions for Green Acres Landscaping.

- **Activity** ----> Students will use the same questions from StartUp Step 22 to complete the INST for their own businesses.

  ----> Print off or make copies of the INST on page 62 to repeat the exercise with fictitious numbers, ensuring that the students learn the order of operations for each of the steps and complete the math correctly.

- **SU Plan** ----> Students will enter the data for their own INSTs into the SU business plan template in their books or online.

Log in to the SUSC to learn more about INSTs, download various templates, and view INSTs by industry. Post your reviews of INSTs for other SUSC members to access.

SU Book, pen/pencil, poster paper, computer, Internet access, SUSC Membership for SU Online Business Plan

INCOMESTATEMENT

ABBREVIATION
INST

Description: *The Income Statement (INST) reports on the amount of revenue a company has earned over a specific period of time. The INST allows the business owner to review detailed information on where the business is making or losing money. The INST is also referred to as the Profit & Loss Statement (P & L).*

Model

Green Acres Landscaping—Monthly Income Statement

Green Acres provides seasonal landscaping services in the southeastern region of the United States. Green Acres' target customer is middle to upper income families. Let's break down Green Acres income statement for the month of June.

Sales: Green Acres made $5,000 in sales.

COS/COG: Expenses for products/services needed to perform the service is $1,000.00.

Gross Profit: Sales-Cost of Goods Sold. After subtracting COS/COG, Green Acres gross profit is $4,000 before subtracting Operating Expenses (OPEX).

OPEX: Fixed Costs + Variable Costs are the expenses the business must pay each month to operate. Total Fixed and Variable Costs to get the Total Operational Costs for the month.

Variable Cost–> Expenses that vary with the amount of product or services sold. A good rule of thumb is to budget 10% for variable expenses. Green Acres VC is $500.00.

Fixed Cost–> USAIIRM expenses that must be paid each month. Green Acres FC is $780.00.

KEEP IT GOING

LEARN MORE ABOUT INCOME STATEMENTS AT WWW.STARTINGUPNOW.COM.

STARTINGUP KEY 22

Profit Less OPEX: Subtracting the OPEX expenses from the Gross Profit will let you know how much revenue the business has generated after OPEX has been paid. In Green Acres' case, OPEX totals $1,280.00.

Charitable Contribution: A portion of the profits a business donates to a charity. This helps the business support not-for-profit organizations in the community and also reduces federal taxes paid. Green Acres also builds *goodwill*, which helps grow its *brand*. Green Acres donates 10% of its profits, or $272.00 in June, to a charity each month.

Profits Before Taxes: Upon subtracting the Charitable Contribution, Green Acres now knows its taxable income that must be paid to the government. Green Acres' taxable income is $2,448.00.

Taxes: Government expenses the business must pay to support the country. Taxes pay for schools, roads, clean water, military, police, and other systems necessary for a country to operate. Green Acres must pay $625.00 in taxes.

Net Profit: The amount the business makes after all operational expenses, charitable contributions, and taxes have been subtracted. This is often referred to as the *Bottom Line* since it's the last line on the INC. This is the amount of money the business owner pays himself/herself, distributes to the ownership, and/or *reinvests* back into the business. Green Acres' net profit is $1,836.00.

INCOMESTATEMENT

Total Revenue			
Sales			$5,000.00
Cost of Goods Sold			$1,000.00
Gross Profit			$4,000.00
Operating Expenses			
Variable Cost (10% of Sales)			$5,000.00
Fixed Costs			$780.00
	Utilities	$50.00	
	Salaries	$500.00	
	Advertising	$0.00	
	Insurance	$50.00	
	Interest	$50.00	
	Rent	$100.00	
	Miscellaneous	$30.00	
Total Operating Expenses			$1,280.00
Profit Less Operating Expenses			$2,720.00
Charitable Contribution (10%)			$272.00
Profit Before Income Taxes			$2,448.00
Income Taxes (25%)			$612.00
Net Profit			$1,836.00

StartUp Step 22: Use the following questions to help guide you through developing an income statement for your business for one month. Use the template on page 58 to record your answers.

1> What are your Sales for this month?

2> What are your COG/COS for this month?

3> Now, subtract your COG/COS from Sales. This is your Gross Profit.

KEEP IT GOING LEARN MORE ABOUT FINANCIAL STATEMENTS AND ONLINE TOOLS AT WWW.STARTINGUPNOW.COM.

4> OPEX
   a. Variable Cost is 10% of your Sales. Determine 10% of your sales and use that amount to budget for your Variable Cost.

   b. Fixed Cost are your OPEX. Use USAIIRM to determine your OPEX.

   c. Add both your Variable Cost + Fixed Cost to get your Total OPEX.

5> Next, you need to subtract Total OPEX from Gross Profit. Put the sum of that amount as your Profit Less Operating Expenses.

6> Now, it's time to determine the amount of your Charitable Contribution, which also reduces your taxable income. We'll use 10% to get started. Determine 10% of your Profit Less Operating Expenses. That's the amount you will donate.

7> Next, subtract the amount of your Charitable Contribution and enter that amount in the Profit Before Income Taxes. That amount is now what your Income Taxes will be based on.

8> Now, it's time to determine the amount of taxes the business must pay. The amount of your taxes is based on the percentage of the business's income. The higher your income, the more you pay in taxes. The lower your income, the less you pay in taxes. For this purpose, let's plan on 25% of your income being taxed. Go ahead and determine 25% of Profit Before Taxes and write that amount in Income Taxes.

9> Finally, to determine your Net Profit, subtract the amount of your Income Taxes from Profit before Income Taxes and that's your Net Profit.

In a traditional Income Statement, charitable contributions are NOT included. However, to encourage donating financial resources to charitable organizations, this has intentionally been included. Please remove this line if you opt to follow a more traditional approach.

Maxim: "I don't like money actually, but it quiets my nerves."
—*Joe Louis, World Champion Boxer*

► INCOMESTATEMENT

ABBREVIATION
INST

Total Revenue			
Sales			
Cost of Goods Sold			
Gross Profit			
Operating Expenses			
Variable Cost (10% of Sales)			
Fixed Costs			
	Utilities		
	Salaries		
	Advertising		
	Insurance		
	Interest		
	Rent		
	Miscellaneous		
Total Operating Expenses			
Profit Less Operating Expenses			
Charitable Contribution (10%)			
Profit Before Income Taxes			
Income Taxes (25%)			
Net Profit			

BALANCESHEET

ABBREVIATION
BAL

[Total Time Required: 45–90 Minutes]

STARTINGUP NOW DESCRIPTION

The **BALANCE SHEET** (BAL) provides the financial position of the business on any given date. It's essentially a "financial checkup" and gives the business owner instant information as to the overall "health" of the business.

NATIONAL STANDARDS FOR ENTREPRENEURSHIP EDUCATION: CONTENT AREA(S) ADDRESSED

- C—Business Foundations
- F—Economics
- I—Financial Management
- M—Business Systems
- O—Strategic Management

- Students will learn how to read and understand a BAL.
- Students will learn the categories, definitions, and order of the BAL.
- Students will to create a BAL for their business plans.

- **Model** ----> Students will read and review Green Acres Landscaping's BAL. The model provides the key learning points and instruction for the students to use in developing their own BALs.

- **Activity** ----> Students will read and learn each of the emboldened definitions and know its function on the BAL.
  ----> Using the chart on page 134 (page 68 for students), students will complete the steps in StartUp Steps 23 as a guide to determine their business assets, liabilities, and net worth.
  ----> Print and/or make copies of the chart from page 134 (page 68 for students) using fictitious numbers to ensure students learn the order and operations for each step. Ensure students complete the mathematical operations correctly.

- **SU Plan** ----> Students will use the financial information from the BAL chart on page 134 (page 68 for students) and enter it into the SU business plan in their books or online.

Review various BAL templates online. There may be industry specific BALs for you to use to structure the BAL for your business. Rate, review, and direct other SUSC members to sites you have found to be helpful.

SU Book, pen/pencil, poster board, copies of chart from page 134 (page 68 for students), computer, Internet access, SU Online

► BALANCE**SHEET**

Description: *The Balance Sheet (BAL) provides the financial position of the business on any given date. It's essentially a "financial checkup" and gives the business owner instant information as to the overall "health" of the business.*

Model

Let's take a look at Green Acres Landscaping's BAL to get an idea of the company's overall health.

Green Acres Balance Sheet—December 31, 2009

	31-Dec	30-Jun
Assets		
Current Assets		
Checking/Savings	$7,962.28	$2,300.00
Accounts Receivable	$200.00	$500.00
Total Inventory Assets	$1,000.00	$2,000.00
Total Current Assets	*$9,162.28*	*$4,800.00*
Fixed Assets		
Equipment	$450.00	$500.00
Computers	$900.00	$1,000.00
Printers	$180.00	$200.00
Telephones	$90.00	$100.00
Total Fixed Assets	$1,350.00	$1,500.00
Total Current & Fixed Assets	*$20,596.53*	*$6,300.00*
Liabilities & Equity		
Current Liabilities		
Accounts Payable	$500.00	$1,000.00
Other Current Liabilities	$500.00	$2,500.00
Total Current Liabilities	*$500.00*	*$2,500.00*
Opening Balance Equity	$20,000.00	$3,800.00
Retained Earnings	$96.53	$0.00
Owner's Equity (Company's Net Worth)	*$20,096.53*	
Total Liabilities & Equity	$20,596.53	$6,300.00

JOIN THE COMMUNITY OF NEW ENTREPRENEURS
AT WWW.STARTINGUPNOW.COM.

Assets: Assets represent ownership of items that may be converted or sold to create cash value.

Current Assets are assets that are usually sold or used up as part of the business operation.

Green Acres' Current Assets as of December 31, 2009

Checking/Savings Account: Cash is considered an asset because of its value. Green Acres Landscaping had $7,962 in its checking/savings account on Dec. 31.

Accounts Receivable (AR): Typically cash that's owed to your company for selling your products/services that's been *Invoiced* to your customer. Most AR has a Net 30 term, meaning payment is due in 30 days. Green Acres has $200.00 in its AR.

Total Inventory Assets: The cash value of your inventory. Green Acres has $1,000 in inventory.

Total Current Assets: Totaling the Checking/Savings Account, AP, and Inventory gives the cash value of your Total Current Assets. Green Acres' Total Current Assets are $9,162.

Fixed Assets are properties that the business owns that can be converted into cash. They are called fixed because they are "nailed" down to the floor.

Green Acres' Fixed Assets as of December 31, 2009

Fixed Assets: Equipment, Computers, Telephone, Printers, Trucks. Green Acres' fixed assets have a cash value of $6,730.

Total Current Assets

Fixed Assets: Provides you with the total cash value of the business. Green Acres has a worth of $15,532.

Liabilities & Equity: A liability is a debt that the business owes. Equity is the value of ownership in the company.

Current Liabilities: Debts the business owes that are to be paid within the year.

Green Acres Liabilities as of December 31, 2009

Accounts Payable (AP): Products purchased or services used by Green Acres for which they owe. Green Acres' current AP is $500.00.

Other Current Liabilities: Consists of expenses that will take longer than a year to be paid, such as a lease or mortgage. Green Acres' Other Current Liability is a $1,500 equipment lease.

Current Equity: The total value of the owner's interest in the company.

Retained Earnings: The amount of cash that's kept in the business and not distributed to owners or shareholders in the company. Green Acres retained earnings is $96.00.

Company Net Worth: The Opening Balance Equity plus the Retained Earnings equals the business's net worth. Green Acres has a net worth of $20,096.

StartUp Step 23: Use the following questions to help guide you in determining your business assets. Record your answers using the chart on page 64.

1> How much will you deposit into your business banking account? Enter that amount under the Beginning Period—Checking/Savings.

2> If you have any current payments that are owed to you, enter that under Beginning Period—Accounts Receivable (AR).

3> If you know the total of your Inventory Assets, enter that under Beginning Period—Total Inventory Assets.

4> Now total your assets to get your Total Current Assets and enter that amount under Beginning Period—Total Current Assets.

5> Follow the same procedure for the following for the Fixed Assets and then total the amount and enter it under Beginning Period— Total Current & Fixed Assets.

KEEP IT GOING
JOIN THE COMMUNITY OF NEW ENTREPRENEURS AT **WWW.STARTINGUPNOW.COM.**

Now, let's determine your business' Liabilities & Equity.

1> Under the Beginning Period column, list any outstanding bills. Total these and enter the amount under Accounts Payable (AP).

2> Under the Beginning Period–Other Current Liabilities, total up any long-term, outstanding debts (longer than 12 months) and enter them here.

3> Now total your AP and Other Current Liabilities and enter the total amount under Beginning Period—Total Current Liabilities

Next, let's determine your ownership stake in the business.

1> Under the Beginning Period column, enter the Opening Balance Equity.

2> Under the Beginning Period column, enter the Retained Earnings. There may not be any earnings since you are just starting.

3> Total Opening Balance Equity + Retained Earnings and you have your Company's Net Worth.

As your business grows, sales will be made and expenses incurred. The BAL will reflect the overall health of your business. Many businesses review their Balance Sheet at the end of each *Fiscal Quarter*. The Balance Sheet provides critical information when analyzing your business growth and progress. It also identifies areas for improvement.

Maxim: "A healthy balance sheet can lead to a restful
and relaxing sleep for the business owner."
—Author Unknown

ABBREVIATION
BAL

	End Period	Beg Period
Assets		
Current Assets		
Checking/Savings		
Accounts Receivable		
Total Inventory Assets		
Total Current Assets		
Fixed Assets		
Equipment		
Computers		
Printers		
Telephones		
Total Fixed Assets		
Total Current & Fixed Assets		
Liabilities & Equity		
Current Liabilities		
Accounts Payable		
Other Current Liabilities		
Total Current Liabilities		
Opening Balance Equity		
Retained Earnings		
Owner's Equity (Company's Net Worth)		
Total Liabilities & Equity		

STARTINGUP KEY 23

KEEP IT GOING — CHECK OUT THE BALANCE SHEET TEMPLATES AND OTHER RESOURCES AT **WWW.STARTINGUPNOW.COM.**

CASH**FLOW**

[Total Time Required: 60 Minutes]

STARTINGUP NOW DESCRIPTION

CASH FLOW (CFLOW) is the movement of cash in and out of the business over a specific period of time. Cash flow helps the business owner track the overall health of the business.

NATIONAL STANDARDS FOR ENTREPRENEURSHIP EDUCATION: CONTENT AREA(S) ADDRESSED

- C—Business Foundations
- F—Economics
- I—Financial Management
- K—Information Management
- M—Business Systems
- O—Strategic Management

- Students will learn the key role that the CFLOW plays in their business operations.

- Students will learn how to complete each of the steps in order to create their own CFLOW statements.

- **Model** ----> Read and review ALG Designs overview. Ensure students understand the importance of accurate financial records—especially when looking to secure a loan or investors.

  ----> Review each of the numbered bullet points for ALG Designs. Students should know the definition and function of numbered bullet points.

- **Activity** ----> Students should use the steps/definitions from ALG Designs CFLOW as a guide to create their own CFLOW. This exercise will likely need to be completed several times using fictitious numbers so students can practice their CFLOW statement.

  ----> Print off or make copies of the CFLOW chart on page 141 to repeat the exercise with fictitious numbers, ensuring the students learn the order of operations for each of the steps. Ensure the students complete each of the mathematical operations correctly.

- **SU Plan** ----> Students will enter the data for their own CFLOWs into the SU business plan template in their books or the SU online template.

Review various CFLOWs online. There may be industry specific CFLOWs for you to edit and incorporate into your business operations. Post your content and share your resources with those in the SUSC network.

SU Book, pen/pencil, copies of chart from page 141 (page 73 for students), computer, Internet access, SUSC Membership to access SU Online Business Plan Template

► CASH**FLOW**

ABBREVIATION
CFLOW

Description: *The movement of cash in and out of the business over a specific period of time. Cash flow helps the business owner track the overall health of the business.*

Model

Sergio Gonzalez has owned and operated ALG Designs, Inc., (ALGD), an Advertising Agency, in Chicago for the past six years. He's grown the company from operating in his basement with 1 client to 17 clients and 5 employees. He's considering opening an office in New York and needs to secure capital for expansion. Potential banks and investors want to review his financial statements, particularly his cash flow, to get an idea of ALGD's financial position. Let's review the Cash Flow statement in detail.

1> **For Year Ending December 31, 2009**—This is the period of time that is covered in the cash flow statement. It provides the exact information of the business's activities during that period.

2> **Cash at Beginning of Period**—This is the total amount of cash the business had on January 1, 2009.

3> **Operating Activities**—ALGD's business activities from January– December 31, 2009.

    a. Net Income—the total amount of income from sales for the specific period. ALGD generated $235,000 in net income.

    b. Cash Paid for—Items listed here are the specific operating expenses broken down by their categories.

        i. Inventory Purchases—Total expenses for inventory purchased for that specific period. ALG Designs spent $50,000 in inventory.

        ii. Operational Expenses (OPEX)—ALG Designs expenses for the business's -operations for that specific period. ALG Designs spent $175,000 in operational expenses.

KEEP IT GOING | VIEW CASH FLOW STATEMENTS BY INDUSTRY AT WWW.STARTINGUPNOW.COM.

      iii. Salaries—the total amount ALG Designs paid to employees for that specific period.

   c. Net Cash Provided by Operating Expenses—to determine this amount do the following: Net Income – Operational Expenses = Net Cash provided by Operating Expenses.

4> **Investing Activities**—the amount of money the business has spent or received from all investment activities.

   a. Cash Receipts from—the amount of income received from the sale of the business's assets.

      i. Sale of Equipment or Property—the amount received from the sale of equipment or property. ALGD sold $15,000 worth of equipment in 2009.

      ii. Sale of Investment Securities—These are typically purchased for investment purposes. Since ALGD needs capital to expand the business, they sold $20,000 worth of stocks and bonds held in other companies.

   b. Cash Paid for—the itemized amount the business paid for physical assets for the business's operations.

      i. Purchase of Equipment—ALGD spent $10,000 on equipment purchases.

      ii. Loans to Others—ALGD loaned $1,500 to a local small business.

      iii. Purchase of Investment Securities—ALGD did not purchase investment securities during this period since they needed cash to expand the business.

   c. Net Cash Provided by Investment Activities—to determine this amount, do the following: Cash Receipts – Cash Paid = Net Cash Provided by Investment Activities.

5> **Financing Activities**—where the business reports the amount of money it spent or received from stocks, bonds, or loans used to finance its activities.

   a. Cash Receipts from Issuance of Stock—this is the amount of cash a business receives if it sold a portion of the business to raise cash. In the case of ALG Designs, Sergio Gonzalez used his own money to finance ALG Designs and still owns 100% of the company. *As long as the owner owns 51% of the company, they control the company.*

      i. ALGD received no cash from issuing any stocks.

   b. Cash Receipts from Loans—is the amount of cash a business receives for any repayments.

      i. ALGD received a $1,000 loan payment in 2009.

STARTINGUP KEY 24

c. Cash Paid for Purchase of Stock—this is the amount of cash a business pays for any stocks or bonds it purchases.

  i. ALGD did not purchase any stock in 2009.

d. Cash Paid for Loan Repayments—the amount of cash a business pays for any loans.

  i. ALGD repaid $10,000 in a loan payment. This also helped reduce their total debt, which is looked upon favorably when seeking investment capital.

e. Dividends to Investors—a dividend is the distribution of profits to owners (shareholders) of the business.

  i. Since ALGD is 100% owned by Sergio Gonzalez, he is entitled to 100% of the profits of ALGD. If Mr. Gonzalez sells a portion of the company—let's say 5%—he would then have to pay the other owners 5% of the profits.

f. Net Cash Provided by Financing Activities—to determine the amount do the following: Cash Receipts – Cash Paid for (Expenses) = Net Cash provided by Financing Activities.

StartUp Step 24: Now that you've had the opportunity to review Sergio's Cash Flow Statement, it's time to create your own cash flow statement based on your business's financial information. If you are just starting your business, you may not have enough financial data needed to generate an accurate cash flow statement. If this applies to you, log on to the StartingUp Skill Center and download sample cash flow statements by industry. This will also help make you aware of the specific Cash Receipts/Cash Paid items you need to add in order to customize your own cash flow statement. This is quite common as you adapt your cash flow statement to your own business or industry. Use the Cash Flow chart above to get started.

KEEP IT GOING
VIEW CASH FLOW STATEMENTS BY INDUSTRY
AT WWW.STARTINGUPNOW.COM.

For Year Ending December 31, 2009		
Cash at Beginning of Period		
Operating Activities		
Net Income		
Cash Paid for		
Inventory Purchases		
Operational Expenses		
Salaries		
Net Cash provided by Operating Expenses		
Investing Activities		
Cash Receipts from		
Sale of Equipment or Property		
Sale of Investment Securities		
Cash Paid for		
Purchase of Equipment		
Loans to Others		
Purchase of Investment Securities		
Net Cash Provided by Investment Activities		
Financing Activities		
Cash Receipts from Issuance of Stock		
Cash Receipts from Loans		
Cash Paid for Purchase of Stock		
Cash Paid for Loan Repayments		
Dividends to Investors		
Net Cash Provided by Financing Activities		

Maxim: "If there is no struggle, there is no progress."
—*Frederick Douglass*

▶ SOLIDIFY THE PLAN

Now that you've completed each StartingUp Key Lesson, use the following template to culminate your own business plan based on what you've learned. Be sure to incorporate your notes from each StartingUp Step as they will serve to assist with your company's development.

Once you've finished each of these sections, enter your information online at www.startingupnow.com using the "Business Plan Template," and then print your complete business plan for presentation.

The end result will be a succinct but detailed plan designed to move your business idea into the marketplace. Be sure to utilize helpful tips, tools, and resources found at www.startingupnow.com.

VAL Incorporate your notes from Step 1 to identify and articulate your company's Core Values.

_____
_____
_____
_____
_____
_____
_____

MST Incorporate your notes from Step 2 to identify and articulate your company's Mission Statement.

_____
_____
_____
_____
_____
_____
_____
_____
_____
_____
_____
_____
_____
_____
_____
_____

STARTINGUP NOW

VIS

Incorporate your notes from Step 3 to identify and articulate your company's Vision Statement. Remember: keep it short.

_____

_____

_____

_____

_____

_____

EXE

Incorporate your notes from Step 4 to identify and articulate your company's Executive Summary.

_____

_____

_____

_____

_____

_____

_____

_____

_____

_____

_____

_____

_____

_____

_____

_____

_____

ESP Incorporate your notes from Step 5 to identify and articulate your company's Elevator Speech.

BIO Incorporate your notes from Step 6 to write your Biography. Tell your story.

STARTINGUP NOW

IDEA — Incorporate your notes from Step 7 to identify and articulate your company's Idea.

_____
_____
_____
_____
_____
_____
_____
_____
_____
_____
_____

LEG — Incorporate your notes from Step 8 to identify and articulate your company's Legal Structure.

_____
_____
_____

MGMT — Incorporate your notes from Step 9 to identify and articulate your company's Management Team.

_____
_____
_____
_____
_____
_____

YOGA

Incorporate your notes from Step 10 to identify and articulate your company's Year One Goals & Activities.

SHORT TERM   LONG TERM

MIA

Incorporate your notes from Step 11 to identify and articulate your company's Industry Analysis.

Incorporate your notes from Step 12 to identify and articulate your company's Marketing Strategy.

STARTINGUP NOW

MARKETING STRATEGY

People:	
Product:	
Price:	
Place:	
Promotion:	
Presentation:	

STARTINGUP NOW

TCP

Incorporate your notes from Step 13 to identify and articulate your company's Target Customer Profile.

FAB

Incorporate your notes from Step 14 to identify and articulate your company's Features and Benefits.

FEATURES	BENEFITS

SELL

Incorporate your notes from Step 15 to identify and articulate your company's Sales Strategy.

COMP

Incorporate your notes from Step 16 to identify and articulate your company's Competition. Use the chart found on page 42 as your guide.

Product:	Local Store	National Chain	Specialty Store

S.W.O.T.S.

Incorporate your notes from Step 17 to identify and articulate your company's S.W.O.T.S.

AD Incorporate your notes from Step 18 to identify and articulate your company's Advertising Message. Don't forget to upload your video as part of your presentation.

_____
_____
_____
_____
_____
_____
_____
_____
_____
_____
_____

SUC Incorporate your notes from Step 19 to identify and articulate your company's Startup Costs.

Item	Unit Cost	Quantity	Vendor	Discount %	Sub-Total

STARTINGUP NOW

OPEX

Incorporate your notes from Step 20 to identify and articulate your company's Operational Expenses.

U-tilities	Budgeted Amount
S-alaries	
A-dvertising	
I-nsurance	
I-nterest	
R-ent	
M-iscellaneous	
Total	

COG

Incorporate your notes from Step 21 to identify and articulate your company's Cost of Goods.

► **INST** Incorporate your notes from Step 22 to identify and articulate your company's Income Statement.

Total Revenue				
Sales				
Cost of Goods Sold				
Gross Profit				
Operating Expenses				
Variable Cost (10% of Sales)				
Fixed Costs				
	Utilities			
	Salaries			
	Advertising			
	Insurance			
	Interest			
	Rent			
	Miscellaneous			
Total Operating Expenses				
Profit Less Operating Expenses				
Charitable Contribution (10%)				
Profit Before Income Taxes				
Income Taxes (25%)				
Net Profit				

Incorporate your notes from Step 23 to identify and articulate your company's Balance Sheet.

	End Period	Beg Period
Assets		
Current Assets		
Checking/Savings		
Accounts Receivable		
Total Inventory Assets		
Total Current Assets		
Fixed Assets		
Equipment		
Computers		
Printers		
Telephones		
Total Fixed Assets		
Total Current & Fixed Assets		
Liabilities & Equity		
Current Liabilities		
Accounts Payable		
Other Current Liabilities		
Total Current Liabilities		
Opening Balance Equity		
Retained Earnings		
Owner's Equity (Company's Net Worth)		
Total Liabilities & Equity		

STARTINGUP NOW

CFLOW

Incorporate your notes from Step 24 to identify and articulate your company's Core Values.

For Year Ending		
Cash at Beginning of Period		
Operating Activities		
Net Income		
Cash Paid for		
Inventory Purchases		
Operational Expenses		
Salaries		
Net Cash provided by Operating Expenses		
Investing Activities		
Cash Receipts from		
Sale of Equipment or Property		
Sale of Investment Securities		
Cash Paid for		
Purchase of Equipment		
Loans to Others		
Purchase of Investment Securities		
Net Cash Provided by Investment Activities		
Financing Activities		
Cash Receipts from Issuance of Stock		
Cash Receipts from Loans		
Cash Paid for Purchase of Stock		
Cash Paid for Loan Repayments		
Dividends to Investors		
Net Cash Provided by Financing Activities		

► SPECIAL**THANKS**

Special Thanks to the following persons who have proven to be faithful friends and colleagues. I appreciate your availability, plethora of skills, and often candid honesty to develop these steps to hopefully serve others whom we may never meet.

Lyman C. Howell, MBA

Vicki D. Frye, Brand & Product Developer
Fryeday Everyday

Mark W. Soderquist, Board Member
The Soderquist Family Foundation

Jenai N. Jenkins, PhD Candidate
Chicago Public Schools

► REVIEWERS

Don G. Soderquist, Senior Vice Chairman and Chief Operating Officer
Walmart Stores, Inc.

Raman Chadha, Executive Director & Clinical Professor
DePaul University, Coleman Entrepreneurship Center

Andre Thornton, Sr., Chief Executive Officer
Global Promotions & Incentives, Inc.

Rev. Dr. Hazel A. King, President & Founder
H.A. King & Associates

Jeffrey Weber, MBA, President,
Jeff Weber Ventures, LLC

Dr. Melvin Banks, Sr., Founder
Urban Ministries, Inc.

Dr. Zira J. Smith, Entrepreneurship and Small Business Educator
University of Illinois-Cook County

Pastor Calvin & Tanya Egler, Founders
Passion Ministries

Dr. Andrea Scott, PhD, Assistant Professor of Marketing
Graziadio School of Business & Management, Pepperdine University

Harold C. Spooner, Executive Vice-President
Covenant Ministries of Benevolence Covenant Church

Pastor Phil Jackson, Founding Pastor
The House Covenant Church

Made in the USA
San Bernardino, CA
25 May 2014